IMPRESSIONS OF THE EAST

IMPRESSIONS OF THE EAST

TREASURES *from the* C. V. STARR EAST ASIAN LIBRARY,

UNIVERSITY OF CALIFORNIA, BERKELEY

DEBORAH RUDOLPH

foreword by PETER X. ZHOU

HEYDAY BOOKS, BERKELEY, CALIFORNIA
C. V. STARR EAST ASIAN LIBRARY, UNIVERSITY OF CALIFORNIA, BERKELEY

Heyday Books and the East Asian Library are especially grateful to Diana Chen of SF Digital Studio, Inc., for the abundance of skill and generosity of spirit that created a book of such elegance and beauty.

PUBLISHED BY HEYDAY BOOKS IN CONJUNCTION WITH THE C. V. STARR EAST ASIAN LIBRARY, UNIVERSITY OF CALIFORNIA, BERKELEY.

© 2007 BY THE REGENTS OF THE UNIVERSITY OF CALIFORNIA
FOREWORD © 2007 BY PETER X. ZHOU
PHOTOGRAPHS © SF DIGITAL STUDIO, INC.

Library of Congress Cataloging-in-Publication Data

Rudolph, Deborah.
Impressions of the East : treasures from the C. V. Starr East Asian Library, University of California, Berkeley / Deborah Rudolph ; Foreword by Peter X. Zhou.
p. cm.
Includes bibliographical references and index.
ISBN 978-1-59714-060-7 (alk. paper)
1. C. V. Starr East Asian Library (University of California at Berkeley)--Catalogs. 2. China--imprints--Catalogs. 3. Japan--imprints--Catalogs. 4. Korea--imprints--Catalogs. I. Title.
  Z881.A12C27 2007
  016.02695--dc22
    2006101811

COVER ART:
  "DAYAN TA FOKE JI TIMING" (SOUTH LINTEL) (PAGE 138)
  "XIPING SHIJING CANSHI" (PAGE 10)
  "ZHANG TIANSHI XIANG BING ZAN" (PAGE 91)

FOR SF DIGITAL STUDIO, INC.
  ART DIRECTION, DESIGN, AND PHOTOGRAPHY: *Diana Chen*
  ADDITIONAL PHOTOGRAPHY: *Walter Swarthout*
  DESIGN: *Susanne Weihl*

ORDERS, INQUIRIES, AND CORRESPONDENCE SHOULD BE ADDRESSED TO:
  HEYDAY BOOKS
  P. O. BOX 9145, BERKELEY, CA 94709
  (510) 549-3564, FAX (510) 549-1889
  WWW.HEYDAYBOOKS.COM

Printed in Singapore by Imago

10 9 8 7 6 5 4 3 2 1

TABLE OF CONTENTS

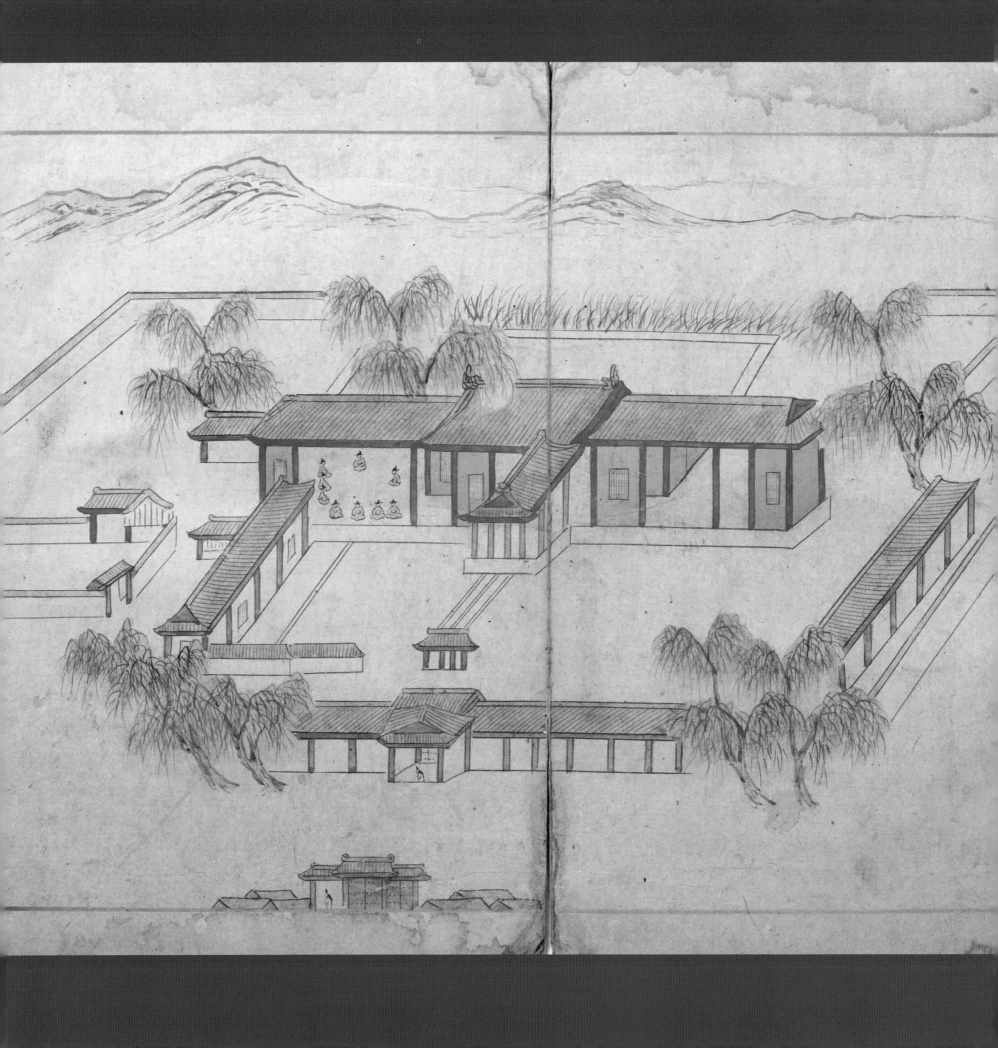

Foreword

Long before Gutenberg printed his Bible, numerous Confucian canonical works, Buddhist sutras, philosophical tracts, belles-lettres, and official documents were being printed and distributed throughout East Asia, birthplace of paper and printing and home to some of the finest woodblock printing ever produced. Chinese, Japanese, and Korean block-printed books first arrived in the United States in the late nineteenth century in the effects of missionaries, travelers, and immigrants returning from the East or emigrating to the West. Many of them seeded what are now some of the largest academic collections of East Asian materials in the country. Those collections grew at an accelerated pace during the twentieth century for reasons ranging from scholarship to geopolitics.

The East Asian Library at the University of California, Berkeley, is one of those collections. This year, 2007, marks the sixtieth anniversary of the East Asian Library's establishment, an auspicious anniversary by the traditional Asian way of counting. Coincidentally, 2007 also marks the Library's move into new quarters, the first freestanding building constructed for an East Asian collection on an American university campus. With the move, the Library will be renamed the C. V. Starr East Asian Library and Chang-Lin Tien Center for East Asian Studies. This book celebrates the occasion and the collection, whose history spans more than a hundred years.

The beginnings of the East Asian collection at Berkeley

The University of California began collecting East Asian materials over half a century before it established the East Asian Library. In 1872, just four years after the founding of the university, a San Francisco lawyer named Edward Tompkins endowed the Agassiz chair in Oriental languages and literature at the university. Tompkins saw that California was already heavily engaged in business with the East; it was "of the utmost consequence," therefore, if this commerce was to develop, that the state be provided with the resources to instruct young residents in the languages and the literature of Asia.

The first Agassiz professorship was offered to John Fryer, a native of England, in 1896. Fryer had lived in China for over thirty-five years. During much of that time, he had worked as a scientific and technical translator at the Jiangnan Arsenal in Shanghai. During virtually all of that time, he had striven to introduce Western science and technology to whatever audience he could. Fryer showed similar energy and dedication at Berkeley. In addition to teaching Chinese, Fryer established what would become the Department of Oriental Languages, now the Department of East Asian Languages and Cultures. He also deposited his personal library on campus, bequeathing it to the university on his death, in 1928. The library contained over two thousand titles, mostly eighteenth- and nineteenth-century imprints, and constituted the beginning of Berkeley's Chinese collections.

In 1914, Kiang Kang-hu succeeded John Fryer as instructor of Chinese at Berkeley, where he also collaborated with Witter Bynner on *The Jade Mountain*, a translation of the popular anthology of Chinese poetry *Tangshi sanbai shou*. After two years at Berkeley, Kiang pledged his grandfather's library of 1,600 titles, in over 13,600 volumes, to the university. The library, which had been reduced to a quarter of its original size during the Boxer Rebellion of 1900, was being stored in a Buddhist temple in Beijing. The U.S. legation shipped it to Berkeley at the request of the university.

The next significant contribution to the collection came from E. T. Williams, who assumed the Agassiz chair in 1918. Williams had served with the State Department in China for more than a quarter of a century and in a number of capacities, including consul general and chief of the Division of Far Eastern Affairs. On his retirement in 1928, he also presented his library to the university.

An important figure in the continuing development of Berkeley's East Asian collection is Horace W. Carpentier. A graduate of Columbia University, Carpentier joined the gold rush to California, where he made his fortune and left his political mark before retiring to New York state. On his death, in 1918, he left over $100,000 to the university, a portion of which University President Benjamin Ide Wheeler earmarked for the purchase of books and materials "relating to the five great areas of Asiatic Civilization." This endowment has been a steady source of funding for the acquisition of Chinese, Japanese, and Korean books for nearly a century.

The collection grew throughout the first half of the twentieth century at a steady pace. Chinese periodicals acquired through a government exchange program were added to the stitchbound classics already among the holdings. From the 1920s, similar exchange programs entered into with Japanese university libraries brought in Japanese publications. By the mid-1930s, the Chinese holdings alone totaled twenty-five thousand volumes. As small as the number is by today's standards, the *New York Times* was sufficiently impressed in 1935 to rank Berkeley's East Asian collection alongside collections at the Library of Congress, the Newberry, and the John Crerar Library. At that time there were other comparable collections in the East, most notably Columbia's and Harvard's, but not another west of Chicago.

The establishment of the East Asian Library

World War II brought Asia into American homes. It also taught America the importance of understanding the language and culture, past and current affairs of its opponents and allies. With the end of the war, East Asian studies programs were established in universities across the country. Concomitant to this was the development of East Asian collections.

Overlooking the Pacific, Berkeley had long been preeminent in East Asian studies. In 1947 the university decided to enhance its standing by establishing the East Asiatic Library (renamed East Asian in 1991). When its first head, Dr. Elizabeth Huff, arrived in Berkeley, the collection consisted of seventy-five thousand volumes housed in various corners of the University Library and scattered throughout its stacks: the Fryer, Kiang, and Williams gifts; a number of Chinese agricultural periodicals and Japanese works on economics and history; the library of Y. S. Kuno, former chair of the department, which focused on the social sciences; works acquired through the Carpentier endowment; a few Mongolian and Manchu titles; and a good selection of Tibetan Buddhist texts. One of the first tasks Dr. Huff undertook was consolidating the collection; another was expanding it.

In 1948, Elizabeth McKinnon, Tokyo-born assistant to Dr. Huff, traveled to Japan to purchase books needed by Berkeley's growing Japanese literature and history faculty. The acquisitions Ms. McKinnon would make on this trip and on subsequent trips would ultimately count among the largest overseas acquisitions undertaken by the Berkeley libraries up to that time. They would also make Berkeley's Japanese collection one of the richest in the United States.

Ms. McKinnon's purchase of the Murakami library brought eleven thousand volumes in literature and the social sciences to Berkeley. Nearly all the titles were first editions dating to Meiji and Taishō, the eras that ushered Japan into the global community and the modern age.

McKinnon's subsequent purchase of one hundred thousand items from the collections of the Mitsui clan increased the Library's rare holdings not only in Japanese but also in Chinese and Korean history, philosophy, religion, letters, arts, and sciences. Newly acquired materials included Japanese books and documents in print and in manuscript; woodblock, copperplate, and manuscript maps; screens and scrolls; and smaller collections of ephemera such as playbills and *sugoroku*, the Japanese board game often compared to parcheesi. The acquisition increased Berkeley's Chinese holdings through the Imazeki collection, compiled by the sinologist Imazeki Hisamaro in the early decades of the twentieth century and purchased from him by the Mitsui; and through Mitsui Takakata's collection of rubbings of Chinese inscriptions and reliefs. The value of another portion of the Mitsui acquisition, the library of early Korean imprints and manuscripts assembled by Asami Rintarō between 1906 and 1918 while serving as legal advisor and judge in Seoul, is inestimable.

The Library's rare holdings were further enriched in later decades by the occasional purchase of unusual items, such as the Ho-Chiang collection of early Buddhist scriptures and the Chen Jieqi rubbings collectively titled *Fu zhai cungu yulu*. The university's ongoing participation in the Farmington Plan, the cooperative acquisitions program launched by American research libraries in the wake of World War II, added hundreds more volumes to the Korean collection.

Rare holdings have also been increased over the years by gifts from members of the faculty, including Woodbridge Bingham of History, Ferdinand D. Lessing of Oriental Languages, and Charles A. Kofoid of Zoology. The Library has been fortunate in receiving rare gifts from friends as well, including William B. Pettus, James Shao-yu Chiang, and Endō Shūsaku. Pettus was a longtime resident of Beijing and president of the College of Chinese Studies in Peking, which moved operations to Berkeley during World War II. James Chiang's grandfather, Chiang Meng-p'ing (Chiang Ju-tsao), amassed one of the finest private libraries in twentieth-century China, Miyun lou. Repeatedly considered for the Nobel Prize in literature, postwar novelist Endō Shūsaku was the recipient of numerous other honors, including the prestigious Akutagawa Prize.

Since the turn of the twenty-first century, the Library has grown at an accelerated rate, spurred by the rising prominence of Asian states in the world's markets and politics and by their increasingly close relations with the United States. Over twenty thousand volumes are added to the Library's collections every year. With print and manuscript holdings totaling well over nine hundred thousand volumes, Berkeley's is now one of the three largest East Asian research collections in the country. It continues to engage in exchange programs with government, academic, and research institutions at home and abroad, and to receive significant support from friends and patrons. The Library has also begun to build a digital collection for East Asian studies in response to the transformation in research and information services brought about by the World Wide Web.

The Center for Chinese Studies Library

The Center for Chinese Studies Library was founded in 1957 as an off-campus reading room affiliated with the university's Center for Chinese Studies and dedicated to the study of contemporary China. The difficulty of obtaining research materials from mainland China in the fifties was compounded by the political atmosphere of the McCarthy era, then only beginning to wane. The reading room offered resources sought by faculty and students and otherwise very hard to come by—publications on the Chinese Communist Party, Chinese society and politics, government, the military, law, and economics. By 1972 the reading room had moved to campus; in the early 1980s it obtained the status of "library." It is now recognized as one of the premier research collections on post-1949 China in the United States.

The Center for Chinese Studies Library's holdings are as various in the perspectives they offer as they are in format and publication type—monographs, periodicals, gazetteers, Party organization histories, recorded television broadcasts, films. Outstanding among these is the series *Wenshi ziliao, Sources for the Study of Literature and History*, over eleven thousand volumes of first-person accounts at the local level of the political movements, military actions, and economic conditions of the late Qing dynasty through the early decades of the People's Republic.

The C. V. Starr East Asian Library and Chang-Lin Tien Center for East Asian Studies

In its early years, the bulk of the Chinese collection was located on the fourth floor of the University Library, in Rooms 416 and 420, with odd titles scattered throughout the general stacks. In 1952, the East Asian collection moved into what had originally been Boalt Hall, Berkeley's law school, and is now known as Durant Hall. Within a decade, the space would prove inadequate: by the 1980s, the East Asian Library had divided its holdings among a number of on- and off-campus sites including, most recently, California Hall and the North Regional Library Facility in Richmond, north of Berkeley. Plans for a new building for the Library were considered over twenty years ago but stalled due to a lack of funding. Interest resumed during Chancellor Chang-Lin Tien's tenure in the 1990s. In 1996, shortly before Chancellor Tien stepped down to resume a teaching career, the C. V. Starr Foundation made the first major donation toward the realization of those plans; architects Tod Williams and Billie Tsien later drew them up.

Named for Cornelius Vander Starr, the former Berkeley undergraduate and insurance entrepreneur who established the Starr Foundation, the new library is located in the heart of campus at the foot of Observatory Hill and across the glade from the Doe Library. Construction was wholly funded by private donations, many given in memory of Chancellor Tien, the first Asian American to head a major research university in the United States. Chancellor Tien's contributions to the Berkeley campus as a researcher, educator, and leader were universally admired. In recognition of his service, which reached back to 1959, as well as his enthusiasm for the new East Asian Library project, the university announced in April 2001 that the East Asian Studies Center at Berkeley, of which the C. V. Starr East Asian Library would form a part, would be dedicated to Chancellor Tien.

With the opening of this new building, the reconsolidated collections of the East Asian Library will merge with the Center for Chinese Studies Library to create a research and learning center equipped to meet the demands of students and researchers in all fields of East Asian studies. In the building itself, the campus will gain an architectural representation of the ideals that have driven Berkeley since its early years: pursuit of excellence, embrace of cultural diversity, commitment to global understanding.

Like the Starr Library and Tien Center, Berkeley's East Asian collection has been built by collective, cumulative effort. *Impressions of the East* documents the success of that effort and is dedicated to all who have been a part of it.

Peter X. Zhou
Director, C. V. Starr East Asian Library
University of California, Berkeley
January 1, 2007

Preface

The purpose of this book is to present selected items from the C. V. Starr East Asian Library's rare book collection in a way that will allow the general reader to appreciate their worth. Part I, "Technical Impressions," discusses books, manuscripts, and rubbings in the collection with reference to the development of printing and publishing in East Asia. Part II, "Cultural Impressions," places further items in the collection in their social, historical, or cultural contexts. The contours of the book follow the idiosyncrasies of the collection; no attempt is made to offer a systematic introduction to the history of printing in Asia or the role of printing in culture or daily life.

Familiarity with Asian culture or history is not needed, although the reader will want to remember that distinctions as well as commonalities existed among the book and printing traditions of premodern China, Japan, and Korea. Geographical proximity of the lands permitted technological innovations to travel. A common written script, classical Chinese, and shared intellectual and religious traditions, Confucianism and Buddhism chief among them, meant that texts often traveled too. At the same time, China, Japan, and Korea individually were able to adopt and modify print technology and cultural institutions and practices in ways unique to each.

In Japan and Korea, for instance, classical Chinese was the written language of officialdom, and knowledge of it the hallmark of a scholar and gentleman. Eventually, however, both Japan and Korea developed scripts of their own, *kana* and *han'gul*, which not only permitted more direct verbal expression in writing but also resulted in higher degrees of literacy among their general populations since the scripts were, unlike Chinese, phonetically based syllabaries. Similarly, in both China and Korea, Confucianism served as the basis of the imperial bureaucracy, while in Japan it was used by the military government, the Tokugawa shogunate, to legitimate its hegemony over the powerless imperial house.

The reader is also asked to note the following conventions. Chinese, Japanese, and Korean names are cited in the traditional order, with surname preceding given name. Dates of Chinese and Korean dynasties and of Japan's prevailing authority, whether imperial or military, can be found in the Chronology. Identifying information provided in the captions refers only to the image reproduced; publication information referring to the original works in which the images appear will be found in the list of Works Featured. Sources for direct quotations will be found in the Sources Cited and Bibliography in the back of the book.

The textual content of an early imprint or manuscript represents only a portion of its worth. Research into its authorship or the circumstances of its production may open a window on past conditions and controversies. Examination of its illustrations may reveal the temperament and character of the people by whom and for whom it was produced. Evidence of past owners and the efforts they took to preserve it may indicate a significance once accorded the text that is otherwise forgotten today. The works discussed in these pages are treasures, not because of the price they would bring at auction, but because of the wealth of interest they hold for us today.

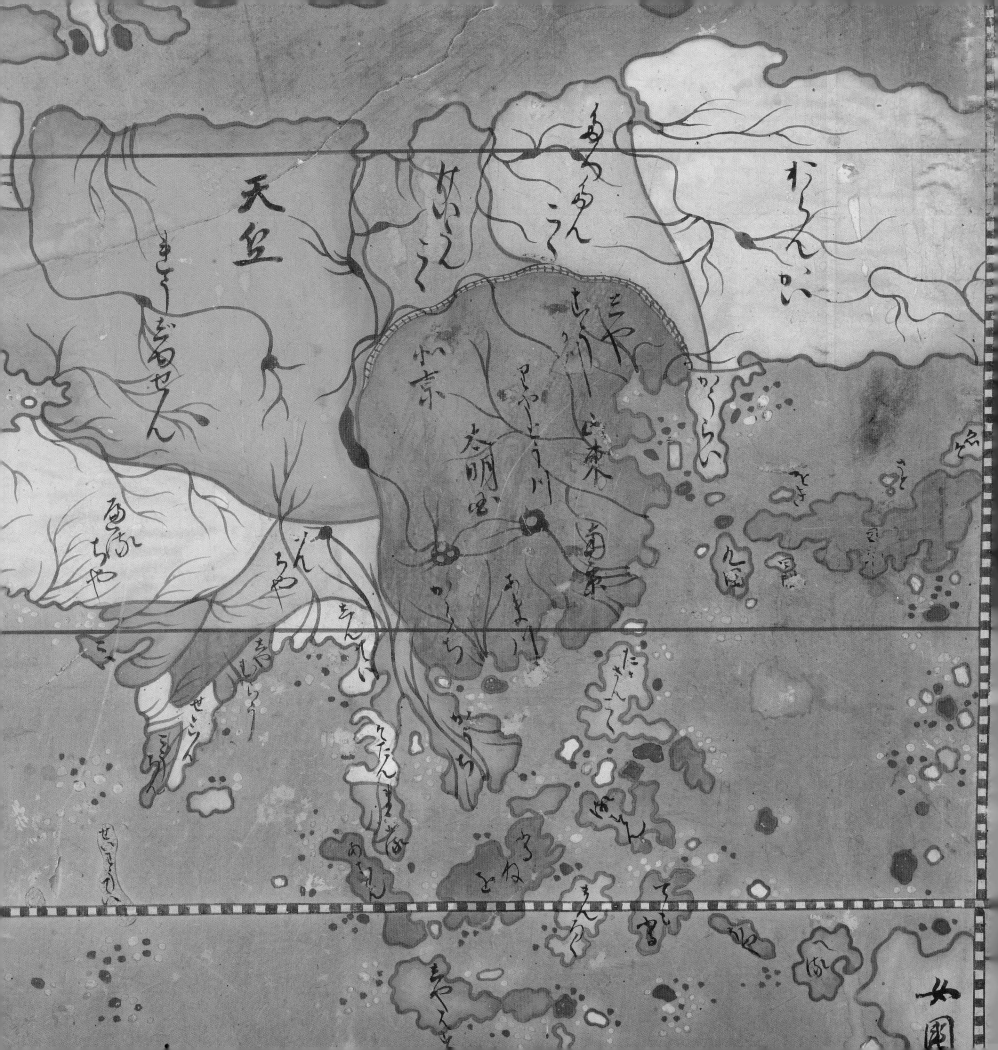

Chronology

China	Japan	Korea
Xia dynasty, 2205?–1766? bc	Jōmon, ca. 10,000–ca. 300 bc	Old Chosŏn, 2333–194 bc
Shang dynasty, 1766?–1122? bc		
Zhou dynasty, 1122?–256 bc		
Western Zhou, 1122?–771 bc		
Eastern Zhou, 770–256 bc		
Spring and Autumn, 722–481 bc		
Warring States, 475–221 bc	Yayoi, ca. 300 bc–ca. ad 250	
Qin dynasty, 221–207 bc		
Han dynasty, 206 bc–ad 220		Three Kingdoms
Western Han, 206–25 bc		Silla, 57 bc–ad 935
Eastern Han, 25–220 ad		Koguryŏ, 37 bc–ad 668
		Paekche, 18 bc–ad 660
Three Kingdoms, 220–80	Kofun, ca. 250–ca. 600	
Jinn dynasty, 266–316		
Northern and Southern Dynasties, 316–589		
Sui dynasty, 581–618	Asuka, 600–710	
Tang dynasty, 618–907	Nara, 710–94	Unified Silla, 668–935
	Heian, 794–1185	
Five Dynasties, 907–960		Koryŏ, 918–1392
Song dynasty, 960–1279		
Northern Song, 960–1127		
Southern Song, 1127–1279		
Liao dynasty, 907–1125		
Jin dynasty, 1115–1234	Kamakura, 1185–1333	
	Kenmu Restoration, 1333–36	
	Ashikaga (Muromachi), 1336–1573	
Yuan dynasty, 1264–1368		
	Momoyama, 1573–1600	
Ming dynasty, 1368–1644		Chosŏn, 1392–1910
	Tokugawa (Edo), 1615–1868	
Qing dynasty, 1644–1912		
	Modern era, 1868–	
	Meiji, 1868–1912	
Republican era, 1912–49	Taishō, 1912–26	Colonial period, 1910–45
	Shōwa, 1926–89	
	Heisei, 1989–	

PART I—*Technical Impressions*

Oracle bone fragment. Ox scapula. Shang dynasty.

Before the market for inscribed bones opened, the peasants of Anyang, Henan, where great numbers of bones were unearthed, sold them to apothecaries, who paid higher prices for unblemished bones. The peasants consequently scraped off any inscriptions they found. Small fragments that were heavily inscribed and therefore difficult to scrape clean were used to fill dry wells. By the first years of the twentieth century, after the market for inscribed bones had established itself, antiquities dealers were faking inscriptions on unmarked bones or padding short inscriptions when price was determined by word count.

Before the Block-printed Book

Shell and bone script

The earliest examples of Chinese script are not written with ink on paper and silk, or on wooden and bamboo slips, or cast into the surface of bronze vessels, weapons, or coins. They are carved into the cracked shells and scapulae of tortoises and oxen. This "shell and bone" script bears only a scant resemblance to the script of today, or even to that of two thousand years ago. It was not even known of by modern scholars until the turn of the twentieth century.

The popular version of the script's discovery, as related by the archaeologist James Mellon Menzies in the 1930s, credits Wang Yirong, a Qing scholar-official with a special interest in bronze inscriptions. One day in 1899, having acquired "dragon bones" from a Beijing apothecary to brew medicine, he noticed what looked like writing on a bone. He bought more bones, studied them, and determined that the writing was an early form of Chinese script. By another contemporary account, an antiquities dealer brought the bones to the attention of Wang. However the inscribed bones first came to light, they have since been the subject of intensive study and scrutiny.

Diviners have used everything from stars to smoke in their efforts to inform a present course of action by looking into the future. The form of divination these bones served, scapulimancy, has been practiced across cultures and continents for thousands of years. It was used in North China as early as the fourth millennium BC.

What distinguishes the oracle bones of the Shang dynasty is the evidence they provide of a more systematic approach to the act of divination, as well as the written record of divination found on the bones themselves.

The Shang diviners heated the prepared shells and bones until cracks appeared. The cracks were interpreted, and occasionally prognostications were made on the basis of the interpretation. Some identifying data were inscribed on the bones before the cracking, but the bulk of the inscription was added to the bone after the cracks had been made, interpreted, and perhaps verified. Very occasionally, the graphs were first written on the bone with brush and ink, then cut into the bone. More commonly, pigments were rubbed into cracks and incisions after the engraving.

In the language of the inscriptions, linguists discern a lexicon and syntax that are already well developed. In the content of individual inscriptions, historians find corroboration for early written accounts of Shang history, including late Shang bronze and jade inscriptions whose accuracy had formerly been questioned or inadequately understood. In the divination records generally, scholars see evidence of a government that appealed to the supernatural for the resolution of political, social, and economic issues.

[OPPOSITE PAGE]

"NEI GONG LI," FROM *FU ZHAI CUNGU YULU*, COMPILED BY CHEN JIEQI. RUBBING AND MANUSCRIPT. 19TH-CENTURY RUBBING OF A ZHOU DYNASTY BRONZE.

In contrast to the oracle bone inscriptions, Zhou bronze inscriptions and script have always been known to scholars, though never fully understood. To ensure accurate transcriptions for study, antiquarians in premodern China collected rubbings of the inscriptions. The nineteenth-century antiquarian Wu Dacheng made this rubbing, taken from a cauldron cast to form part of a young woman's dowry.

內公匜
舊釋太公
王廉生農部
釋作芮

SEALS

Today we use strings of numbers, barcodes, and microchips to assure others of our creditability. In early China, seals were used for the same purpose. Gan Yang, Ming dynasty compiler of the catalog of early seals *Jigu yinpu*, writes that the Chinese character for "seal," *yin*, is made up of two components: one signifying the act of clutching or grasping, the other signifying insignia. Together, they mean to hold in the hand insignia that demonstrate trustworthiness. The analysis is paraphrased from China's first etymological dictionary, *Shuowen*.

Some historians link the need to authenticate identity with the emergence of commercial centers and private landholding between the eleventh and third centuries BC, but archaeologists have found seals predating that time. The more commonly held view accordingly points to the general need for security and confidentiality, especially in matters concerning governance, diplomacy, and warfare.

The seals used in pre- and early imperial China were made of various types of metal and stone, of ivory, horn, even earthenware and wood. Metal seals were cast, but those made of other materials were carved. They were generally, though not always, square. Their inscriptions were usually brief. Originally used to impress clay, early seals tend to be carved in intaglio to produce a raised impression, although relievo carving was common enough by the fifth to the third centuries BC. The earlier examples tend to be official seals, of interest to scholars for what the place-names and titles occurring in the inscriptions might reveal about institutional history and administrative geography. Because of the occasional imposition of sumptuary laws, even the material the seals were made of can be of interest to historians as well as collectors of antiquities. Epigraphers study early seals, whether official or private, in tracing the development of the written script.

Historians of technology and the development of printing view the carving and use of seals as logical antecedents to woodblock printing. Conceptually, the purpose of both seals and woodblocks is to duplicate text. Technically, seals of stone, horn, and wood shared certain commonalties with the printing block: they were carved; their texts were engraved in reverse and in relief; and from the first century, if not earlier, seals were inked to make their impressions on paper. The Chinese collective consciousness must have agreed that a link existed between the two techniques: with the introduction of woodblock technology, the word for seal, *yin*, came to be used for the act and art of printing.

[OPPOSITE PAGE]

Gu shi Yihai lou cang yinkuan niu tuoben, COMPILED BY GU YUAN. RUBBINGS AND HAND-PRESSED SEALS. 19TH-CENTURY IMPRESSIONS OF A QING SEAL.

Antiquarians and scholars have been compiling catalogs of seal inscriptions since the Song dynasty. As a rule, the inscriptions were simply recarved on the woodblock for printing. Occasionally, the collector-compiler would produce a small edition in which the seal inscriptions were duplicated by pressing the seals themselves, whether originals or reproductions, onto each page. The collector Gu Yuan went one step further, including rubbings of each seal's top or side surfaces as well.

新莽壓戟郡連率銅虎符

"YARONG JUN HUFU," FROM *FU ZHAI CUNGU YULU*, COMPILED BY CHEN JIEQI. RUBBING AND MANUSCRIPT. 19TH-CENTURY RUBBING OF A BRONZE DATING TO AD 9–25.

Tiger tallies were another early way to authenticate identity. Cast in two interlocking parts, this bronze tiger bore an inscription along its spine. On arriving at his destination, the messenger or envoy presented one-half of the tally to his host, who held the other half. If the two parts fit and the halved inscription became whole, the messenger and his message could be trusted. The tiger tally reproduced in this rubbing was cast for official use in Yarong commandery during the Xin dynasty of Wang Mang, in the early decades of the Christian era.

"Xiping shijing canshi."
Ca. 19th–century rubbing of a
Song or Ming recarving of an
ad 175 engraving.

*Seven years after they were erected, the
Xiping stone classics were damaged during a rebellion. Although the stones were
ordered repaired and sections recarved, by
the sixth century some had been lost and
others so badly damaged that they were
being used as building material. Hundreds
of fragments of the stones survive today,
though none is bigger than the surface of
a school desk. The fragment reproduced by
this rubbing is engraved with portions of
the "Great Plan" chapter of the* Book of
Documents, *and is probably taken from a
Song or Ming recarving.*

"Cheji tu." 20th-century
rubbing of a Later Han relief.

*The tomb reliefs of Sichuan, which have
come through the centuries in better
shape than the stone classics, offer another
window on the Han dynasty. While some
reliefs portray mythological beings or
historical events, many depict everyday
life at all levels of society. There are scenes
of hunting and harvesting, feasting and
entertainment, marketplaces and private
homes. Here, the sort of cart that might
have choked the streets of Luoyang.*

Stone inscriptions

Having achieved the political unification of China, the first imperial dynasty, the Qin, began the process of cultural unification. Its successor, the Han, took unification further, adopting Confucianism as the state orthodoxy and requiring all who would participate in governing the state to gain proficiency in its precepts and principles.

With such a requirement in place, the textual integrity of the core works of the Confucian canon became a matter of concern to more than a handful of scholars. It became critically important to the instructors at the imperial academy, the training ground for the civil service, as well as to their students, who by the late first century BC numbered in the thousands. Until the late second century AD, there were only two ways the text of the canon could be transmitted, by manuscript and by memory, and both were susceptible to error, omission, and deviation.

In AD 175, during the Xiping era, a group of scholar-officials petitioned the throne to have a standard version of the canon established. Once this was done, the emperor ordered leading calligraphers of the day to write out fair copies of the texts and their commentaries. These copies were used to engrave the texts on forty-six stone slabs, which were erected at the imperial academy in the capital at Luoyang in the year 183. The purpose was to have an authoritative text in a durable medium and in a place not only accessible, but accessible to a number of readers at once. According to the *History of the Later Han*, so many came to see the stones that their carts choked the streets of the capital.

Students and scholars could read the erected stones in place. They could use the inscriptions to collate and amend manuscript copies of the texts already in their possession. They could write out copies of their own while standing before the stones. Tradition has it that they also duplicated the engraved text by making ink rubbings of the inscriptions. Modern scholars discount this tradition for the simple and unarguable reason that paper samples surviving from the second and third centuries are too coarse to have been effectively used for rubbings. There is clear evidence, however, that the technique was in use by at least the sixth century.

To make a rubbing, dampened paper is placed over an engraving, tamped with a stiff brush, then patted all over with an inked pad. The smooth surface of the stone is replicated on the paper in ink; where the stone has been incised and the paper tamped into the incision, the paper remains white. As a method of duplicating text, the process is quick, accurate, and cheap. There are obvious technical differences between printing from a woodblock and taking a rubbing from stone. The woodblock is carved in relief, while the stone is incised. The carved text of the woodblock is reversed, while the stone inscription is not. And the woodblock is inked, while in making a rubbing, the paper itself is inked.

More significantly, perhaps, is the nature of each technique as an undertaking. The Xiping stones were intended not as simple tools for the replication of text but as monuments to cultural tradition. Even if they might later prove vulnerable to the hazards of war and weather, at their creation they were intended to be immutable and enduring. At completion, their scale and sponsorship made them essentially public pronouncements of the place of Confucianism in Chinese government and society, even if later historians of the development of printing would characterize them as tools for the replication of text.

A MILLION PRINTED CHARMS

The first texts known to have been printed in Japan, the *Hyakumantō darani*, "Million Pagodas Dhāranī," were the byproduct of a clash between religion and politics. The annalistic history *Shoku Nihongi* records the manufacture and distribution to various temples, in 770, of one million three-storied pagodas of diminutive size. Inside the hollow core of each was placed one of four *dhāranī*, or charms. The stated reason for this act was thanksgiving for the restoration of peace after civil strife in the eighth year of the Tempyō-hōji reign, 764. Other early sources specify that the project was begun in 764 and only completed in 770, and that ten temples received the pagodas, including Tōdai-ji, in Nara, and Hōryū-ji, to the north of Nara.

Nara was the site of both the central government of eighth-century Japan and the most powerful Buddhist temple in the empire, Tōdai-ji. Along with other Buddhist temples and monasteries, Tōdai-ji had profited from the tax exemptions and relaxed restrictions on land tenure granted it by the imperial government. As imperial favor deepened, the temples' wealth and influence grew, until eventually the Buddhist clergy became not only a presence but a power at court. By some, it was even considered a threat. Among them was the Fujiwara clan.

The Fujiwara were well-established members of court and shapers of policy and law, as well as providers of imperial consorts and empresses. Emperor Junnin, installed just a few years before the manufacture of the miniature pagodas, was a Fujiwara son-in-law who had succeeded to the throne when his aunt, Empress Kōken, abdicated. Following the custom of the day, Kōken entered a Buddhist convent on retirement, but she never renounced her involvement in the world or her ambition on behalf of her spiritual advisor—some say lover—the monk Dōkyō. Alarmed at the monk's mounting influence, Emperor Junnin's father-in-law staged a revolt, the civil strife of 764. In the course of the revolt, Junnin's father-in-law was killed; in its aftermath, Junnin was deposed. Kōken reascended the throne as Shōtoku, and Dōkyō was soon appointed chief minister. In the estimation of some historians, Shōtoku's printing project was an attempt to placate the Buddhist clergy as much as to give thanks for peace.

Prayers and sutras are commonly reproduced as an act of devotion. The sutra from which the *Hyakumantō* charms are taken specifically directs the devotee to make multiple copies of charms and place them in pagodas. In the case of Shōtoku's *dhāranī*, the act was mechanically assisted: the pagodas were turned on a lathe, and the charms were printed. Exactly how they were printed, whether by woodblock or metal plate, has been argued by experts for years, with no firm conclusion. To paraphrase one expert, the scale of the printing is too great to have been undertaken without experience, but the execution too crude to attest to experience. Close examination has yielded clues but no answers. The discovery of a woodchip argues for block printing; the absence of the signs of wear that would accrue on a woodblock argues for metal plate.

Until the 1966 discovery of another charm dating to sometime before 751, at the temple Pulguk-sa, in Kyŏngju, Korea, the *Hyakumantō darani* were thought to be the earliest specimens of printed text in East Asia.

Hyakumantō darani. Wood,
metal plate or woodblock.
764–70.

The Jishin'in darani *is one of six charms*
included in the sutra Mukujōkōkyō.
According to the sutra, recitation or
repeated copying of the charms will
alleviate illness, prolong life, and assure
salvation. Unlike the empress, court
ministers trusted action over prayer,
banishing Dōkyō after Shōtoku's death,
in 770, and barring women from
succeeding to the throne. They also moved
the capital from Nara to put distance
between court and clergy.

獻頌曰

佛以大圓覺充滿河沙界我以顛倒想

出没生死中云何以一念得往生淨土

我造無始業本從一念生既從一念生

還從一念滅生滅滅盡處則我與佛同

如投水海中如風中鼓橐槖有大聖智

亦不能分別願我先父母與一切眾生

在處為西方所遇皆極樂人人無量壽

無往亦無求

魚枕冠頌一首

瑩淨魚枕冠細觀初何物形氣偶相值

忽然而為魚不幸遭網罟剖魚而得枕

方其得枕時是枕非復魚魚湯火就模範

巉然冠五岳方其為冠時是冠非復枕

成壞無窮已究竟亦非冠假使未變壞

送與無髮人簪導無所施是名為何物

我觀此幻身已作露電觀而況身外物

露電亦無有佛子慈閔故願受我此冠

WOODBLOCK IMPRINTS

THE BLOCK-PRINTED LEAF

An open leaf from a block-printed book can illustrate, perhaps more clearly than an image of the book itself, how woodblock volumes were printed and put together. The leaf reproduced here represents two pages from a Song dynasty edition of the collected works of one of China's most eminent scholars and statesmen, Su Shi, also known as Su Dongpo.

This leaf would have been printed from a single block. After the block had been soaked, polished, and otherwise prepared for engraving, and a copyist had written out on paper the text to be engraved, the paper would have been pasted facedown on the block, leaving a mirror impression of the text once the excess paper had been rubbed off. The engraver would first have carved all vertical lines in the text, then all horizontal and diagonal lines and all the dots. For economy's sake, both sides of the block might be carved.

To print, printers inked the block and applied paper to it, brushing the back of the paper to ensure an even impression before pulling off the printed leaf to dry. Once dry, the leaf was folded in half, creating two pages. Folded leaves were gathered together and sewn to form a volume, most commonly with the folds forming the vertical fore-edge of the volume and the open ends, stitched, forming the spine.

The slender column in the middle of the leaf, the "heart of the block," marks the fold. The ornament in the heart that resembles two triangles side-by-side, the "fishtail," would have served as a guide for folding. Printed in the heart of the block under the fishtail is the same sort of information the modern reader finds in a book's running heads: abbreviated title, chapter number, page number. Since these are printed right where the leaf is folded, in the finished book they would be semi-legible, literally, from either page. The leaf pictured here also has the name of the engraver at the bottom of the heart, as most Song imprints would. Engravers' names were included on the blocks to aid in calculating the amount of work done by a particular engraver and therefore the amount of money due him by the publisher. Occasionally, even the character count was engraved at the bottom of the block.

Some features of this leaf's design are common to Chinese imprints of any dynasty and any printing house: the borders around the text and the double borders to the left and right; the lines separating columns of text; the broader margin above the text, the "heavenly brow"; and the narrower margin below the text, the "earthly foot."

Other features are characteristic of Song printing from Sichuan. Sichuan was an early center for printing in China; the industry was concentrated in Chengdu, long the political and economic center of the region, and in Meishan, downstream from Chengdu. The proportions of both the characters and the page layout are generous, even grand. The calligraphy, at once simple and stately, is modeled after that of the Tang calligrapher Yan Zhenqing. The printed page presents a balance of black and white that is aesthetically dignified without being cold or lifeless. The text is printed on white hemp paper, manufactured in Sichuan and valued for its durability, fine texture, and flawless whiteness.

[PAGE 14]

Su Wenzhong gong wenji, by Su Shi. Woodblock. Southern Song dynasty.

After centuries of thumbing and paging, the fold of this leaf has worn through. Even so, it is a treasure. Su Shi's writings were proscribed at one point in his professional career, making any Song printing of his work rare. Imprints from Sichuan are scarcer still, since the larger printing establishments of Meishan and Chengdu were destroyed by Mongol invaders at the end of the Song dynasty, eliminating the possibility of later issues being printed from the Song blocks.

DATING ENGRAVING AND DATING PRINTING

It is generally said that about fifteen thousand leaves could be printed from an engraved woodblock, and another ten thousand after the block had been touched up. Printing blocks carved for a book with a limited market might be used for centuries. The modern bibliographer attempting to determine the publication date of an early imprint must therefore answer two questions: when the blocks were carved, and when the impression was made.

In the absence of a printer's colophon that might answer these questions, the bibliographer can examine the body of the text for clues to the date of the carving. In imperial China, for instance, the personal names of reigning emperors, and perhaps even those of their sons and senior male relatives, were avoided in speech and writing out of respect or fear, or simply in acknowledgment of the sovereign's superior status. The "taboo" could be observed a number of ways in print, such as omitting a stroke from the forbidden character or using a synonym or homonym in its place. During the Song dynasty even homonyms were avoided, the taboo was so strictly observed.

Engravers' names may appear in the heart of the block, further refining the possible date of printing. By comparing editions whose printing history is well established, historical bibliographers have been able to identify the floruit dates of certain engravers. Names dating to different dynasties would indicate that worn blocks were recarved sometime in the book's history. Often this is specifically indicated with the notation *bu*, "to supplement, repair," appended to the later printers' names.

A survey of the page design may corroborate the suggestion that the book was printed from blocks carved at different times. All leaves in the book known to be printed from Song blocks, for instance, may have a single border at top and bottom and a double border at the sides enclosing the text, in a page design characteristic of later Song printing, while other leaves are printed with a double border at all four sides. The height of the printed text area on the leaves may vary, as may the calligraphy and ornamentation.

Further research in documentary sources, including whatever prefaces or afterwords are included in the volume, can fill in details, such as whether a work was reprinted, or what necessitated the recarving of certain blocks. Bibliographers may learn more about the date of a printing by comparing the copy in question with other known copies of the same edition, but the sort of basic examination of a text summarized here can be practiced by any reader.

DONGLAI LÜ TAISHI WENJI,
BY LÜ ZUQIAN. WOODBLOCK.
1204–1644.

Standard reference sources note that the collected works of the literatus Lü Zuqian were engraved onto printing blocks in 1204. Although the observance of a Song dynasty taboo in the copy pictured here suggests it might have been printed from the 1204 blocks, variations in ornamentation and engravers' dates, discrepancies in text area, calligraphy, and the quality of the printing all indicate that the blocks from which these pages were pulled were engraved at different times. The annotation bu *in the lower left of the left-hand page supports this.*

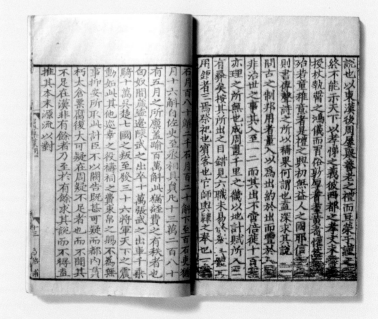

大般若波羅蜜多經卷第五百二十六

第二分九方便善巧品第二十六之四　　三藏法師玄奘詔譯

爾時善現復白佛言世尊常訖甚深般若波羅蜜多甚深般若波羅蜜多依何義故名為般若波羅蜜多佛告善現由此般若波羅蜜多到一切法究竟彼岸依此義故名為般若

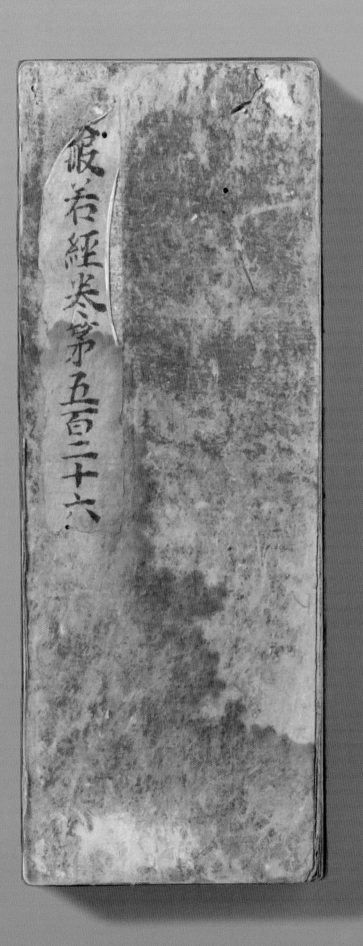

般若經卷第五百二十六

DAIHANNYA HARAMITTA-KYŌ. WOODBLOCK. EARLY 13TH CENTURY.

During the early Kamakura period, it became customary to present Kōfuku-ji imprints at a nearby Shinto shrine dedicated to Kasuga-myōjin and associated with the Fujiwara clan. These imprints came to be called Kasuga-ban, or Kasuga imprints. Early Kasuga-ban were known for the high quality of their paper, ink, and calligraphy. The paper was frequently gampi, or "goose skin," which is naturally insect-resistant, strong, smooth, and lustrous. The ink was a deep, rich black. The calligraphy was forceful. Here, a Kasuga-ban of the Sutra of Great Wisdom.

TEMPLE PRINTING

The production of a million *dhāraṇī* at the order of the empress Shōtoku in 770 should have marked the beginning of the development of printing, especially religious printing, in Japan. Yet there is no extant evidence of further printing projects until 1009, when a thousand copies of the Lotus Sutra were printed, according to the diary of a member of the Fujiwara clan. The earliest extant text printed subsequent to the Shōtoku *dhāraṇī*, a scriptural commentary known in Japanese as *Jōyuishiki-ron*, dates to 1088. Why no texts were printed between the time of the empress's charms and the Lotus Sutra is uncertain.

It is unlikely that the technology was somehow lost, since the closely related technique of stamping was in use during the printing hiatus. The concept of producing texts by block printing was also known in Japan during the interim between the *dhāraṇī* and the Lotus Sutra through Buddhist monks who had traveled to China in search of teachers or scriptures and returned to Japan with Chinese imprints. Printed scrolls and books, both religious and secular in nature, were regularly imported from China as well through the luxury trade.

This has led some scholars to suggest that texts were printed between the late eighth and eleventh centuries, even if none have been preserved. Others have suggested that printing was not practiced simply because there was no perceived need for it: literacy was limited before 1600, and the replication of sutras for devotional reasons still required hand copying, in spite of the example set by Shōtoku.

Once printing reappeared in Japan, it remained for centuries wholly the domain of the great temples of Kyoto and Nara, the Zen monasteries of Kyoto and Kamakura, and a handful of provincial temples. Monks worked as copyists, engravers, printers, and binders; sutras and doctrinal works formed the bulk of their production; temple patrons provided the necessary funding. The wealthier the temple and its patrons, the greater, very often, its printing activity. It follows that the family temple of the Fujiwara, the Kōfuku-ji of Nara, was a prolific center of printing. The *Jōyuishiki-ron* of 1088 was, in fact, a Kōfuku-ji imprint.

While the temples of Kyoto produced religious texts at the request of patrons seeking spiritual merit, the Nara temples, particularly the Kōfuku-ji, broadened the scope of printing in Japan by producing texts for the practical purpose of propagating Buddhist teachings. By the time Nara printing was in decline, in the late fourteenth century, the Zen monasteries had become centers of printing, broadening the scope of publishing further still by producing non-Buddhist works, from Chinese classics to medical treatises. This expansion of the purpose of publication, the subject matter, and the readership must subtly have contributed to the loosening of the Buddhist hold on printing that concluded with the introduction of movable type at the end of the sixteenth century.

Jianben fuyin Chunqiu Gongyang zhushu, traditionally attributed to Confucius and Gongyang shi, annotated by He Xiu, Xu Yan, and Lu Deming. Woodblock. Ming dynasty printing from Yuan dynasty engraving.

Chapter opening from the Gongyang commentary to the Spring and Autumn Annals, *an early history whose authorship has traditionally been ascribed to Confucius. The larger characters represent the text of the history, the smaller characters, the commentary. This page was printed from one of the original blocks carved under the sponsorship of the Yuan Directorate of Education: the engraver Ying Yu (or Wang Yingyu), whose name appears in the lower left, is known to have been active during the Yuan dynasty and to have carved blocks for other directorate printings of works in the Confucian canon.*

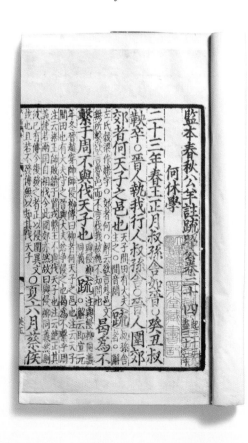

GOVERNMENT PRINTING

While the Buddhist imperative to proselytize influenced and accelerated the development of printing in China, Chinese temples never monopolized publishing as their Japanese counterparts did. Private individuals, as well as religious bodies, funded the printing of sutras in ninth-century China, and by the last decades of the century the private and unauthorized printing of calendars had been officially and disapprovingly noted. By the early years of the tenth century, the central government was sponsoring publication projects as well.

The same need that brought the Han court to inscribe the Confucian canon in stone, the need for an authoritative version of the canon for the education of future government officials, brought the Later Tang court to order the printing of the canon in 923. By decree, the base text was the stone inscription of the canon then on display in the capital. The editors were instructors from the Directorate of Education, the copyists carefully chosen. The engravers were charged with carving five woodblocks a day.

In succeeding eras, the Directorate of Education continued to publish works needed for training the young men who would become the empire's elite. Other bodies within the central government—the directorates overseeing medicine, astronomy, official translation, the palace library, the treasury—all issued their own imprints, as did less ostensibly learned government bodies, such as the commission controlling the tea and salt monopolies. Further down the bureaucratic scale, government offices at the provincial, prefectural, and county levels sponsored their own printing projects.

The growing practice of government publication was not interrupted during the Mongol Yuan dynasty. In fact, the Yuan Directorate of Education's printing of the Confucian canon (mistakenly identified as Song imprints by later collectors) served as base texts for numerous subsequent editions of the thirteen classics. The Qing scholar-official Ruan Yuan used them as the base for his recension of the canon, *Shisan jing zhushu,* published while Ruan was serving as governor of Jiangxi.

By the fourteenth century, the subject matter of government publications had extended far beyond Confucian classics, administrative manuals, and dynastic records to include non-canonical classical literature, Buddhist and Daoist texts, even popular fiction and drama. During the Ming dynasty, editorial and publishing projects were used to distract imperial princes from forming seditious ambitions. During the early Qing, they were used to lull Ming loyalists into allegiance. Politically expedient as they were, however, the monumental projects of the Yongle, Kangxi, and Qianlong reigns were also undertaken, like the first directorate printing of the Confucian canon, with the objective of preserving and disseminating the learning and literary heritage of the past.

QINDING GUJIN TUSHU JICHENG, COMPILED BY CHEN MENGLEI AND
JIANG TINGXI. BRONZE MOVABLE TYPE AND WOODBLOCK. 1726.

*In the 1720s the government's Imperial Printing Office, the Wuying dian, printed
sixty-six copies of the encyclopedia* Gujin tushu jicheng, *with woodblock illustrations
and typeset text. The bronze type—two hundred and fifty thousand characters—was
eventually melted down for coinage.*

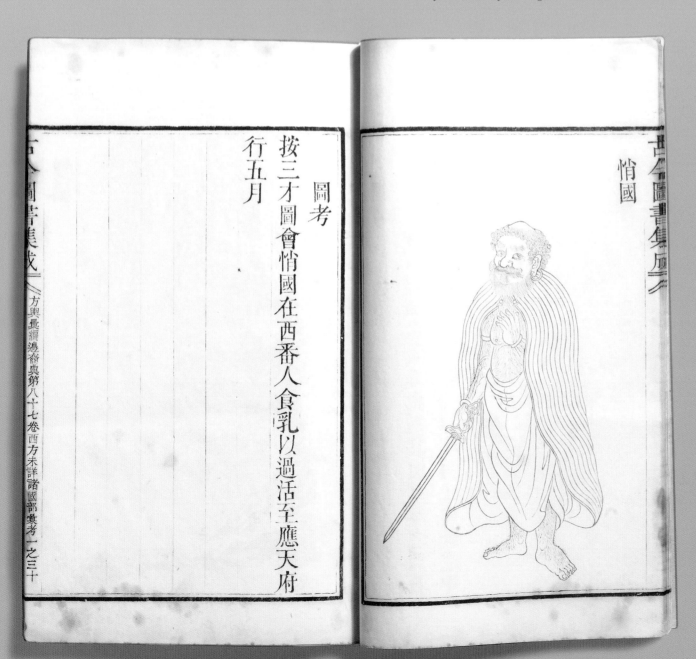

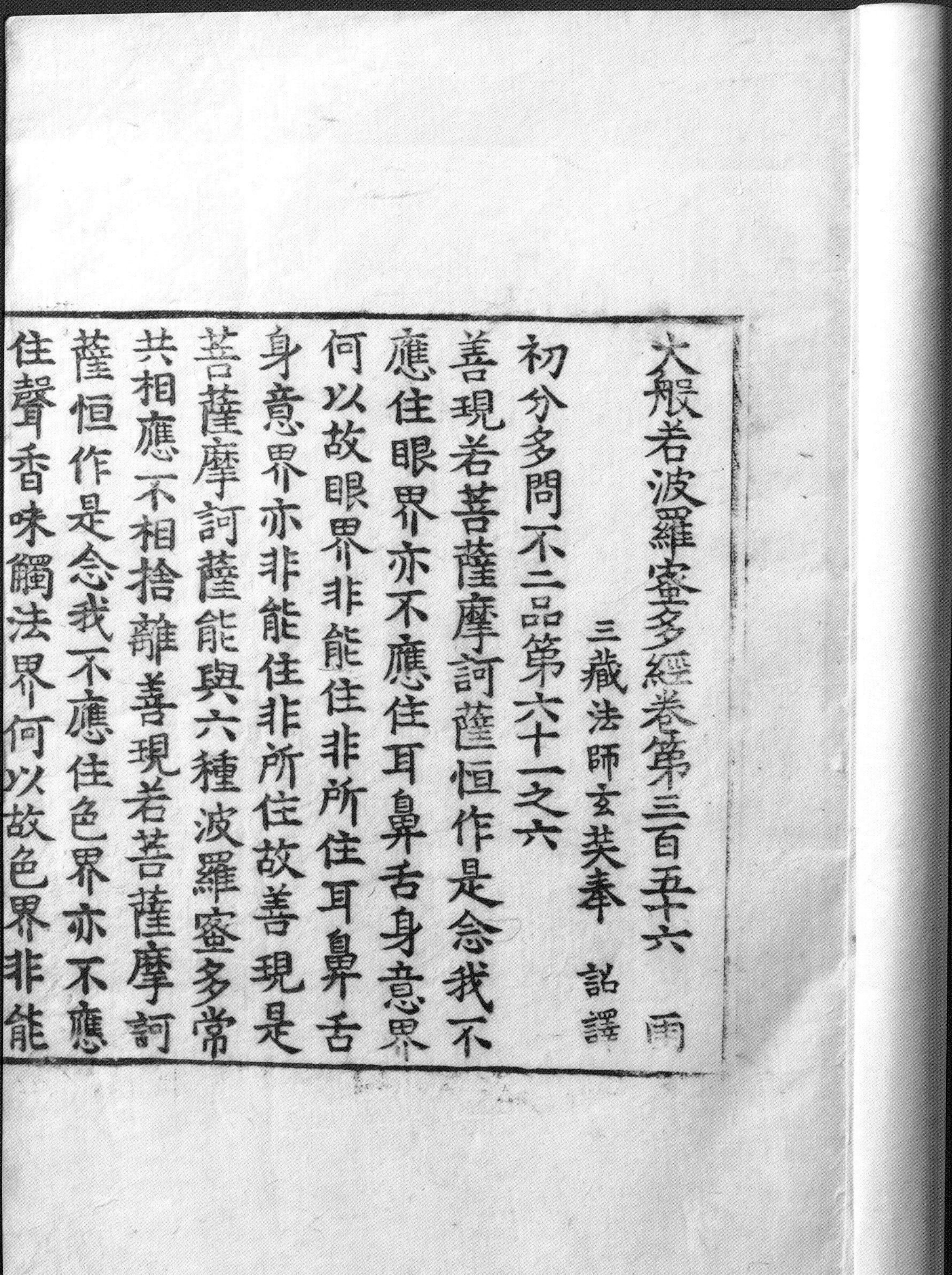

六般若波羅蜜多經卷第三百五十六　雨

三藏法師玄奘奉　詔譯

初分多問不二品第六十一之六

善現若菩薩摩訶薩恒作是念我不

應住眼界亦不應住耳鼻舌身意界

何以故眼界非能住非所住故善現

身意界亦非能住非所住故善現是

菩薩摩訶薩能與六種波羅蜜多常

共相應不相捨離善現若菩薩摩訶

薩恒作是念我不應住色界亦不應

住聲香味觸法界何以故色界非能

Taebanya paramilta kyŏng.
Woodblock. 1238.

The monks of the Haein-sa still occasionally print from the thirteenth-century blocks stored there. Crucial to the blocks' preservation are the temple's storerooms, whose design ensures optimal temperature, humidity, and airflow. The temple entered Unesco's World Heritage List in 1994. Here, a page from the Sutra of Great Wisdom, printed from the Haein-sa blocks.

Printing and diplomacy

Intellectual copyright disputes and the lost profits that generate them aside, it is difficult in the twenty-first century to imagine the prominent role the technology of printing played in foreign relations in earlier ages, a role that is portrayed dramatically in the history of printing in Korea.

The earliest extant example of printed text in Asia is a sutra found on the grounds of a Buddhist temple in Kyŏngju, capital of the Korean kingdom of Silla. While the origins of the printing are hotly disputed—some scholars maintain that it is Korean, others that it is Chinese—the existence of a commerce in books between China and Korea is not in dispute. Since at least the tenth century, and possibly as early as the eighth, Korea was importing from China Buddhist texts and occasionally blocks used to print such texts. The Korean kingdom of Koryŏ also imported Confucian canonical works, Chinese official histories, and medical treatises. While no objection seems to have been voiced to the exportation of religious texts, at the end of the eleventh century members of the Chinese ruling elite petitioned the throne to halt the trade in secular works, fearing it would threaten the national security of China vis-à-vis Korea and its Khitan allies.

A nomadic people who controlled the periphery of northern China between the tenth and eleventh centuries, the Khitan were also the impetus behind the first large-scale printing project begun and completed on Korean soil. This was a printing of the Korean Buddhist canon, executed in fulfillment of a vow sworn by the king and ministers of Koryŏ in 1011. In 1009, a bloody coup at the Koryŏ court had concluded with a regicide and the enthronement of a compliant successor. In retaliation for the murder of their former ally and vassal, the Khitan sent an army of four hundred thousand across the Yalu River to march on the Koryŏ capital. The new king and his supporters made their vow in the face of this onslaught and in hope that the act of devotion would invoke divine aid.

Ten years of sporadic warfare ensued, ending with victory on neither side but a resumption of the tributary alliance that had once joined the adversaries. The printing of the canon, which required the engraving of thousands of woodblocks, was completed in 1082. A supplement of almost equal size was undertaken in 1101. The blocks prepared for both were burned in the chaos of the Mongol invasion of Korea in 1232. Another vow was sworn, another canon engraved, on eighty thousand printing blocks. These blocks survived; they are now housed at the Haein-sa, in South Kyongsang Province, South Korea.

DAIHANNYA HARAMITTA-KYŌ.
WOODBLOCK. 1384.

Most copies of the first Buddhist canon printed in Korea were destroyed or have disappeared. The Diamond Sutra shown here, printed in 1384, was possibly based on a copy of the sutra that survived in Japan. Facsimile editions were produced by pasting the leaves of a copy of the original work, or a traced copy of it, onto new blocks, then engraving in the usual way.

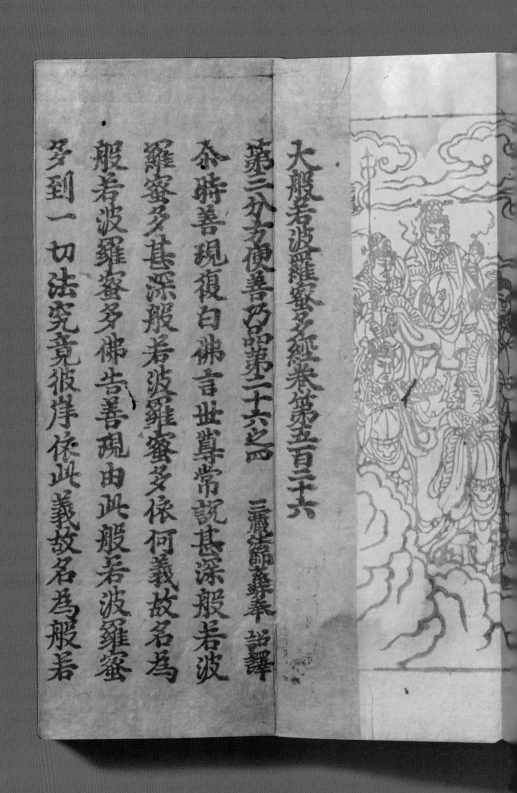

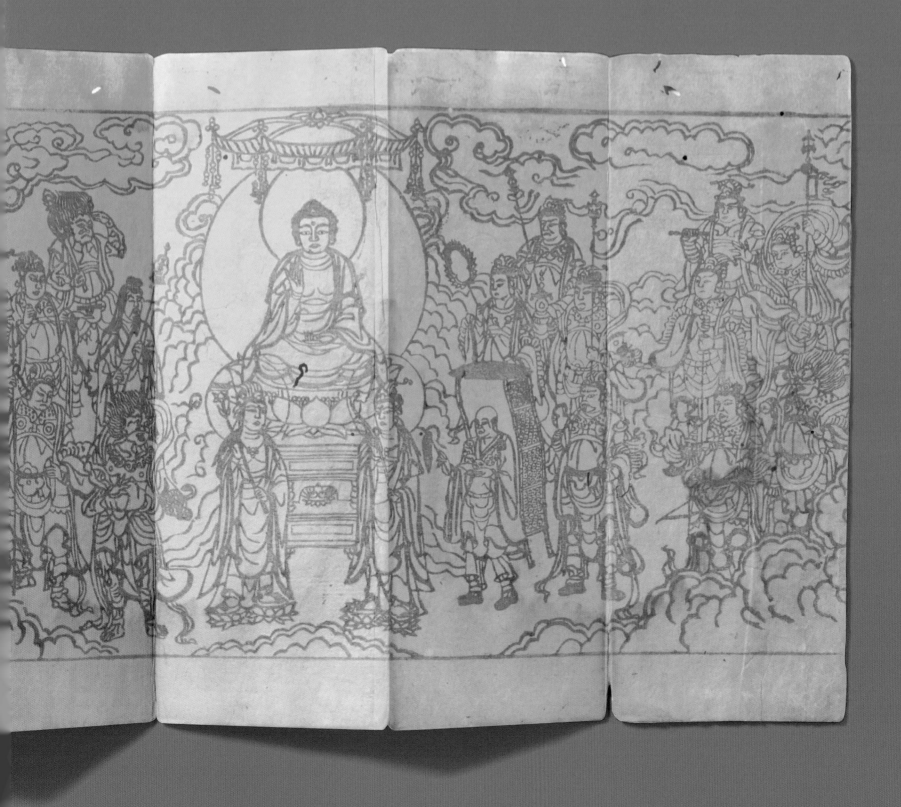

WOODBLOCK ILLUSTRATION

Thanks to the pictographic element in Chinese script, the technical ability to reproduce images emerged in step with the ability to reproduce text. Thanks to the power of images to instruct, amuse, and delight, that technical ability continued to develop over the centuries.

Until the sixteenth century, there had been no discernable division of labor between illustrator and engraver, or much credit given to either. Publishers of the late Ming, however, understood that the success of the illustration depended on the skill of the artist no less than that of the engraver. This change in attitude can be ascribed to the competition of the marketplace, the aesthetic sensibilities of the Ming, or simply the natural maturation of the art. Whatever the reason, as the sixteenth century unfolded, regional styles began to assert themselves, exceptional engravers began to earn not only acknowledgment but recognition for their work, and publishers began to engage professional artists as illustrators. The trend continued into the Qing dynasty, when even the occasional literatus-painter, like Chen Hongshou, was employed to execute the drawings that would be engraved and printed.

The early twentieth-century bibliophile Zheng Zhenduo pointed to the importance of technical skill to the overall quality of woodblock illustration in his memoir of book hunting, *Jiezhong de shu ji*. He owned a reprint edition of the *Chu ci, Songs of Chu*, with illustrations by Chen Hongshou, but had never seen a copy of the original edition. When he finally obtained one, what caught his admiration was less the artist's genius than the engraver's and printer's expertise: "The hairs and whiskers were as fine as silken threads, as black as if touched with lacquer."

Modern critics praise the 1879 edition of *Honglou meng tuyong* along similar lines. A collection of portraits of characters in the novel *Dream of the Red Chamber, Honglou meng tuyong* is frequently cited as proof that Qing printing can vie with the best of the Ming. A comparison of the 1879 edition against one of its later reprints demonstrates as well that no matter how striking the original design, its successful translation into woodblock illustration depends as much on the engraver's skill and the printer's craft as on the artist's brush.

HONGLOU MENG TUYONG, ILLUSTRATED BY GAI QI. WOODBLOCK. 1879.

It is generally held that the quality of Chinese woodblock printing declined during the Qing dynasty, and to such an extent that dealers resorted to pricing Qing illustrated editions the same way horses are measured, by the span of one's hand. Works like the original edition of Gai Qi's Honglou meng tuyong, *lacking neither art nor craft, suggest that late Qing and Republican era collectors gave more weight to a book's relative antiquity than to its appeal and execution. Gai Qi's seal appears in the lower right.*

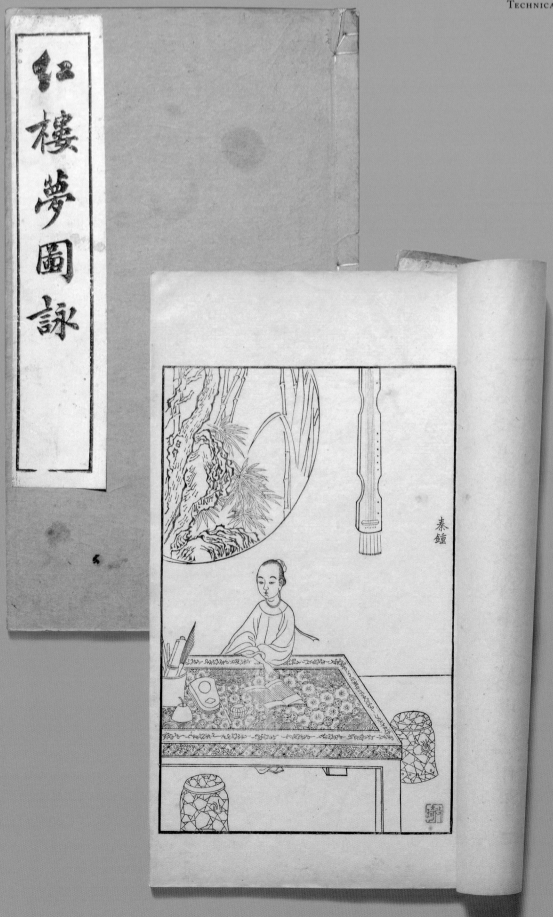

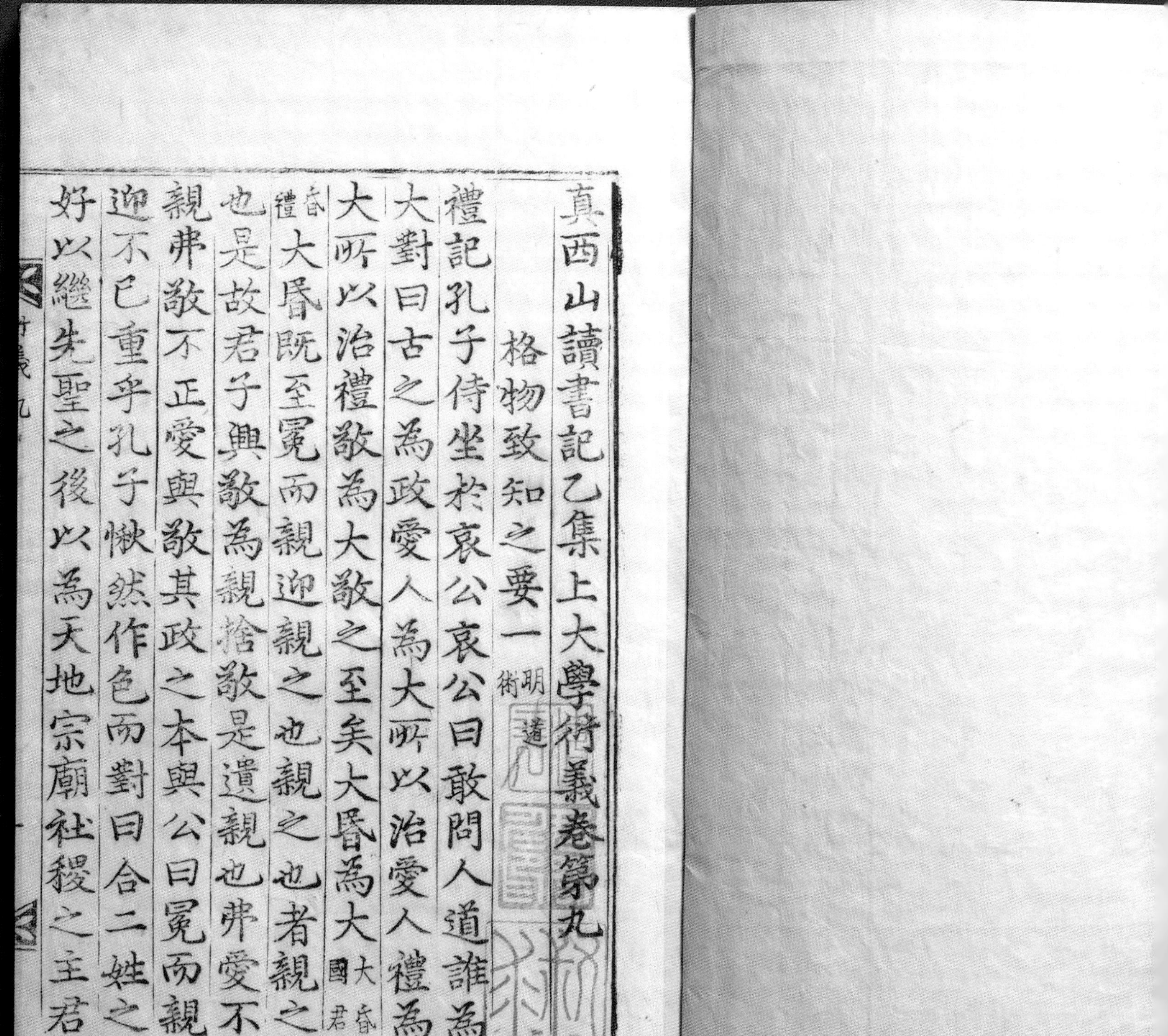

真西山讀書記乙集上大學衍義卷第九

禮記孔子侍坐於哀公哀公曰敢問人道誰為
大對曰古之為政愛人為大所以治愛人禮為
大所以治禮敬為大敬之至矣大昏為大
大昏既至冕而親迎親之也親之也者親之
也是故君子興敬為親捨敬是遺親也弗愛不
親弗敬不正愛與敬其政之本與公曰冕而親
迎不已重乎孔子愀然作色而對曰合二姓之
好以繼先聖之後以為天地宗廟社稷之主君

Variations in Print

Metal movable-type printing

In Korea, as in China, the central government was quick to recognize the valuable role printing could play in fostering Confucianism and the civil service that was founded on it. As long as civil service examination candidates depended on manuscript copies of the Confucian canon, textual variation and error would threaten common understanding. Texts printed from a single authoritative version of the canon, however, would unify the vision of the governing class and ensure the supremacy of the orthodox way. In China, this reasoning led the government to sponsor printing projects using existing woodblock technology. In Korea, it spurred the development of movable-type technology.

China had been exporting books to Korea through both private and diplomatic channels since the early centuries of the Christian era. This trade came to an official, if not de facto, end when the Chinese literatus Su Shi urged the throne not to permit the sale of Directorate of Education texts to the Korean envoy then at court. His fear, which was shared by others, was that the intellectual exchange would dangerously strengthen Korea and its Khitan allies to the point where they might threaten China's already precarious borders. When the Chinese Northern Song dynasty did fall not long thereafter, in 1126, Korea was forced to develop print technology of its own.

The Chinese had experimented with earthenware movable type in the eleventh century, and later with wooden and metallic type. But type never found favor in China, at least not on a large scale.

By the early thirteenth century, on the other hand, Korea had developed the mold and casting processes that allowed the mass manufacture of metal type. During the early fifteenth century, Korean officials acting on the king's command improved the method used for fixing type in its chase, thereby greatly increasing the efficiency of the printing process and enhancing the aesthetic quality of the printed page. Throughout the century, the royal foundry continued to design and cast new fonts in different calligraphic styles.

Scholars have identified factors that might have led Korea to adopt movable type technology where China had rejected it. Korea lacked the plentiful supply of hardwood needed for woodblock engraving, and Korea had an alphabet, *han'gŭl*, better suited to typography than the myriad characters of the Chinese lexicon. But movable type was used to print works in Chinese, not *han'gŭl*; and any office or institution falling outside the central government's monopoly on the technology—temples, private schools, even local government offices—was forced to depend on woodblock technology to print sutras, textbooks, and government manuals. The central government's desire to promote orthodox thought is the overwhelming factor in Korea's use of movable type, but it is an ambivalent one: while the government supported the development of print technology, it suppressed the growth of commercial publishing, which would have diminished the power of the government's voice but spurred the further development of typography and printing.

[PAGE 28]

CHINSŎSAN TOKSŎGI ULCHIPSANG TAEHAK YŎNŬI, BY ZHEN DEXIU. METAL MOVABLE TYPE. 17TH CENTURY.

This Korean edition of the Chinese Neo-Confucian work Daxue yanyi *is exemplary of the close relationship between the central government and printing. In an appendix, the publisher, the Government Printing Office, chose to reprint postfaces concerning fonts developed by the royal foundry in the early decades of the fifteenth century.*

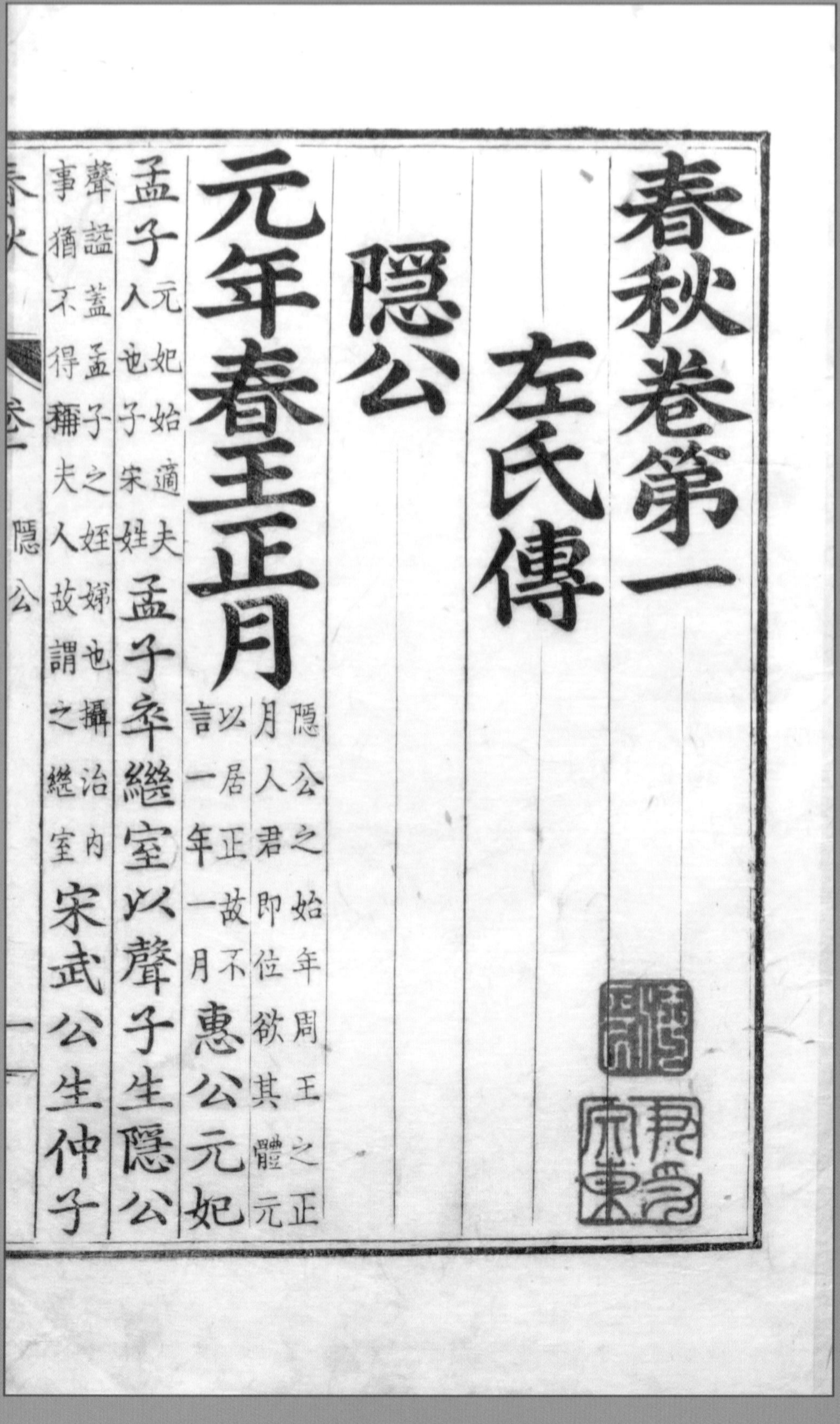
春秋卷第一
左氏傳
隱公
元年春王正月隱公之始年周王之正月人君即位欲其體元以居正故不言一年一月惠公元妃
孟子元妃始適夫人也子宋姓孟子卒繼室以聲子生隱公
聲諡蓋孟子之姪娣也攝治內事猶不得稱夫人故謂之繼室宋武公生仲子
春秋 卷一 隱公 一

Ch'unch'u Chwa ssi chŏn, traditionally attributed to Confucius, annotated by Zuo Qiuming, edited by Yi Sŏ-gu. Woodblock and movable type. 1797.

According to a postface, this Korean printing of the Confucian classic Spring and Autumn Annals, *with commentaries by Zuo Qiuming and later scholiasts, incorporates two different technologies. The commentaries were printed in movable type cast from a copper alloy, while the borders, the title and chapter headings, and the main text—the large characters—were printed by woodblock. The size of the large characters probably dictated the use of wood. Woodblock allowed the larger characters to breach the upper inner border, emphasizing the visual and moral weight of the classic's words.*

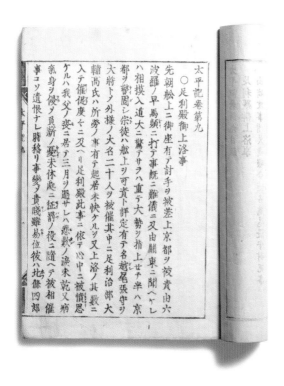

TAIHEIKI. WOODEN MOVABLE
TYPE. 1610.

The broad appeal of A Record of the
Great Peace *made it one of the earliest
examples of Japanese literature printed
by movable type and one of the most
frequently reprinted and reissued.
Unusual among movable-type imprints
published by neither temple nor court,
this edition has a printer's colophon identifying the year of publication as 1610 and
the publisher as "Shunshi"—possibly a
merchant, possibly a private printer,
working either alone or in association
with a temple turned printing center.
The white-on-black trefoil ornament in
the left margin, at the fold, is a direct
borrowing from contemporary Korean
printed books.*

WOODEN MOVABLE-TYPE PRINTING

In the spring of 1592, Japanese forces invaded Korea, swiftly taking the capital at Seoul and sending the royal court into flight. A year later, these forces were just as quickly withdrawn in the face of a Chinese army advancing in response to Korea's appeal for aid. The imperial regent Toyotomi Hideyoshi was nonetheless able to present the Japanese emperor with spoils of war, including printing presses and the metal fonts favored by the Koreans.

On receiving the Korean fonts, the Japanese emperor ordered the printing of the Confucian *Classic of Filial Piety*. He then ordered wooden type cut for the printing of a number of other imperial editions, chiefly of Confucian classics and chiefly in Chinese. While temples experimented with typeset editions of Buddhist sutras, also in Chinese, private individuals began to engage in printing ventures of their own. Once types for the Japanese syllabaries, *hiragana* and *katakana*, had been developed, Japanese literary classics were printed alongside other works that might be of interest to the educated samurai class.

Unlike the Koreans, the Japanese came to favor wooden type over metal. Some ascribe this to the expense of casting the tens of thousands of Chinese types that would be necessary for any printing project; others attribute it to the abundance in Japan of cherry, a fine-grained hardwood ideal for engraving. In Korea, wood was used for type only when metal was in shortage, in times of war or when trade with Japan broke down. Japan had a good supply of copper, however. Japan also had the technical expertise, both in principle—the Japanese were skilled metalworkers— and in fact—type was cast in Japan to supplement that brought back from Korea (tradition attributes this foundry work to typecasters brought back by Hideyoshi's forces).

Hideyoshi died in 1598, five years after his forces returned from Korea. Tokugawa Ieyasu, who succeeded him as de facto ruler of Japan, proved to have a strong interest in printing, ordering fonts cast and cut, and sponsoring the printing of movable-type editions. In spite of his influential patronage and the spread of the new technology, as literacy spread and the demand for books grew, the economics of the marketplace dictated that the woodblock be re-employed. Fifty years after it was introduced, movable-type printing was abandoned, although the secularization and vernacularization of printing in Japan would continue to gain momentum.

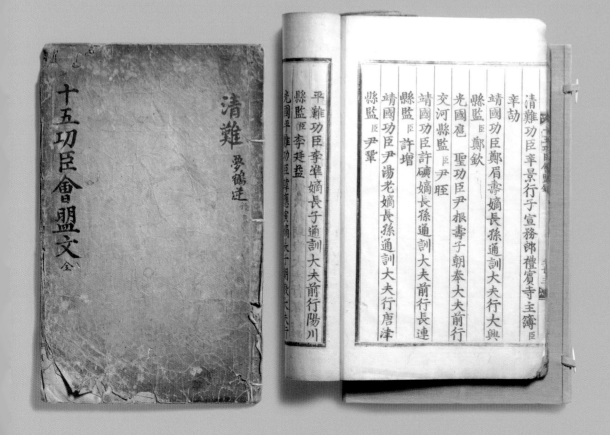

KANJE SIJIP, BY CHEN YUYI.
WOODBLOCK. 1544.

*Collectors will recognize the square
Japanese seal on this Korean edition of
the Chinese literatus Chen Yuyi's poetry
as the seal of Tokugawa Yoshinao, son of
the shogun Ieyasu. It is commonly found
on Korean imprints looted in 1592 that
subsequently entered Ieyasu's, and later
his son's, personal library.*

SIBO KONGSIN HOEMAENGMUN.
METAL AND WOODEN MOVABLE TYPE.
EARLY 17TH CENTURY.

*Because of the metal shortage that typically
accompanied war, the Korean type lost to
Japanese plundering was not easily
replaced. In the years following the
Japanese retreat, Korean printers made
do by mixing metal type with wooden
type modeled on it. Here, a Government
Printing Office volume printed with such
a mix, commemorating the meritorious
service of named officials during the
Japanese invasion and its aftermath.*

Ligatured movable type

In the twenty-first century, aesthetic concerns may seem to lag behind technological advancement, but during the era of *kokatsujiban*, early movable type editions, they arguably spurred the development of Japanese print technology.

At the time Korean moveable-type fonts were introduced into Japan, three scripts were in use there: Chinese characters, or *kanji*, and the two Japanese phonetic syllabaries, *hiragana* and *katakana*. Because the first fonts introduced were Chinese-character fonts, the first movable-type imprints in Japan were naturally Chinese classics and certain Japanese works written in Chinese. After fonts had been developed for *hiragana* and *katakana*, however, works incorporating both *kanji* and *katakana* were printed, followed by works incorporating *kanji* and *hiragana*.

In terms of calligraphic style, the Korean fonts first used in Japan employed the standard script style, *kaisho*, sometimes referred to as the "box" style, since every *kanji* is written inside an imaginary square box. The advantages to the typographer are obvious—discrete graphs that lend themselves to orderly columns and rows. Other calligraphic styles are less typographically docile, especially the "grass" or cursive style known in Japanese as *sōsho*. In origin, *sōsho* was the abbreviated form of writing that court scribes used when taking notes. It quickly developed an aesthetic of its own, one that resonated especially with Japanese sensibilities. It is hardly surprising therefore that within years of learning the basics of movable-type printing, Japanese printers were developing cursive fonts for *hiragana* as well as *kanji*.

There is a form of cursive calligraphy, *dokusō*, in which each character is unconnected to the characters above and below it in a column of text. During the *kokatsujiban* era, however, *renmentai*, the form of cursive that calls for ligatures between characters or *hiragana* and *katakana*, was also popular. The thin line linking one graph to another suggests speed, spontaneity, and fluidity, while demonstrating the calligrapher's absolute control of his brush and ink. Setting ligatured type presented a challenge to printers—ligatured types could be two to three times the size of unligatured types—and yet it was done. Although one historical bibliographer has argued that developing ligatured type was a matter of linguistic imperative, it is commonly assumed that the printers' impetus was aesthetic, an attempt to reproduce in print the beauty and vitality of the handwritten script.

Ironically, aesthetic concerns also contributed to the abandonment of movable-type technology in seventeenth-century Japan. When the demand for illustrated works increased, printers found the woodblock a more hospitable medium for pages presenting both text and illustration. They also found it an economically more practical medium for producing a small number of works in a generous variety of calligraphic styles.

EIGA MONOGATARI. WOODEN MOVABLE TYPE. 1624–43.

Written in a combination of hiragana *and* kanji *sometime after 1092,* A Tale of Flowering Fortunes *adopted a more conversational tone than earlier Japanese histories, which had been written in Chinese and according to Chinese historiographical principles. The first line on the right, below, provides an abbreviated form of the chapter title and is a good example of ligatured type. The two* kanji *form a proper noun,* Kazan, *the name of the Yamashina temple also known as* Gangyō-ji. *The three* hiragana *that open the text form a single word,* kakute, *"thus." Later readers have added reading marks in red, notes in brown, and the page number, in the lower left, in black.*

Dai Nihon saiken dōchū zukan,
by Chisokukan Shōkyoku.
Woodblock with color. 1876.

*In the early days of Japanese commercial
map publishing, maps were printed in
black and hand-colored, if colored at all.
By the 1770s, they were being block-
printed in color. An alternative technique,
first employed in the 1760s, used stencils to
add color to black and white maps. The
regular misalignment and occasional
puddling of some of the colors applied to
this map suggest stencil-coloring.*

Hand-colored woodblock illustration

The Japanese prints that came to the general notice of the West in the late nineteenth century and so fascinated the French Impressionists represented a technical tradition directly descended from woodblock printing and book production.

Illustration became a common feature of Japanese block-printed books in the seventeenth century, at just the time the temples lost their monopoly on printing and the stability provided by the newly established Tokugawa shogunate allowed the development of a middle class and a proportionate rise in the rate of literacy. Works outside the narrow confines of the Buddhist and Confucian canons were being offered for sale, and there was a public waiting to buy them. Illustrations that were added to enhance or elucidate text proved to be selling points. And because one technique was used to produce both text and illustrations, the latter were easily included in the printed book, and even incorporated into the printed text.

Based on line drawings and printed with the same ink as the text, these illustrations lent themselves to hand-coloring. The earliest examples, the "red and green" *tanroku* editions, were limited in color and hastily execut-ed. But other examples of hand-colored illustration exhibit a palette and precision that make them indistinguishable, for the average viewer, from polychrome woodblock illustration of the eighteenth century.

Commercial publishers had begun to employ professional artists as illustrators in the last decades of the seventeenth century. At the turn of the eighteenth, they found a ready market for these illustrations independent of their bibliographical context. Initially, the single-sheet prints were sold as they had been printed, in black on white. Soon they were being hand-colored as the book illustrations were. By mid-century, the method of using multiple blocks to produce a single color print of the type shown at the Paris exposition of 1867 was being used in Japan for both illustrations and prints.

Rikka hiden shô. Woodblock with hand-coloring. 1688.

Symbolism in Rikka-style flower arrangement was expressed through design and plant selection rather than color. To the uninitiated, however, hand-coloring gives this illustration an attraction it would not have had in its original uncolored state.

Suizoku shashin, compiled and illustrated by
Okugura Tatsuyuki. Color woodblock with mica. 1855.

*The coloring in this 1855 work on snapper is block-printed, although so
subtly that the book is frequently described as hand-colored. Powdered
mica has been added to the page to simulate the sheen of the fish's scales.*

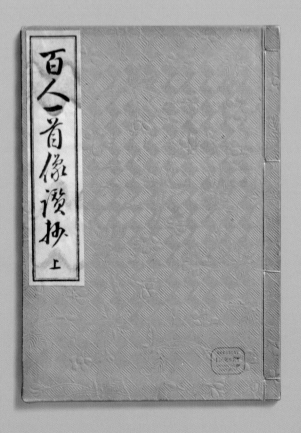

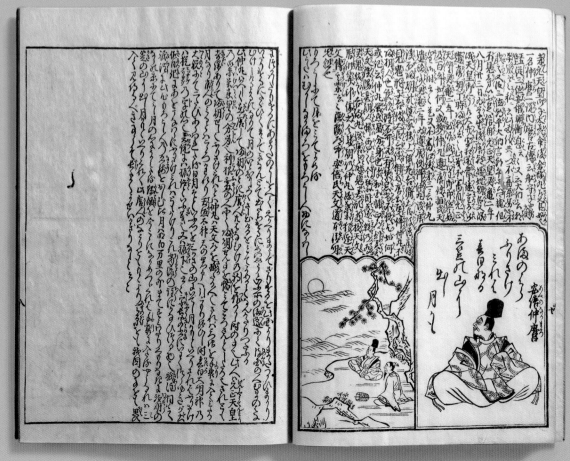

Hyakunin isshu zōsan shō, by Nakanoin Michikatsu, illustrated by Hishikawa Moronobu. Woodblock. 1683.

The poet Abe no Nakamaro recalling the sight of the moon over Mikasa-yama, by Hishikawa Moronobu. Prolific, versatile, a painter as well as an illustrator, Moronobu worked in a number of styles. He produced his illustrations and prints—he is said to have been the first artist to produce prints—in black on white only. Some were subsequently hand-colored by their owners.

40 |

Cheng shi moyuan, compiled by Cheng Dayue. Woodblock and single-block color woodblock. 1606.

Although the early attempt to print polychrome illustrations from a single woodblock is well documented, few examples of such printing remain. Some survive in a handful of copies of Master Cheng's Catalog of Ink Cakes. *Cheng Dayue had selected illustrations printed in color in a small number of copies of his ink catalog. As this illustration demonstrates, the more detailed the engraving, the more difficult the inking during printing.*

COLOR WOODBLOCK ILLUSTRATION

Polychrome woodblock printing was practiced in China at least as early as the seventeenth century. Before that time, text might be printed in multiple colors to distinguish commentary from principal text; a sutra printed in black might be accompanied by an illustration printed in red; illustrated books printed in black might subsequently be colored by hand. But the use of three or more woodblocks to produce a single polychrome illustration was not a feature of book production.

Chinese publishers and printers began to experiment with polychrome woodblock illustration during the Ming dynasty. In early trials, inks of different colors were spread on a single block, from which one impression was taken. The method became messy when a fuller palette was used and the boundaries between areas of color were fine and proximate.

Printers then tried extending the process used for black-and-red printing, carving separate blocks for each color. This could require the engraving of up to ten blocks, twenty blocks, or more for a single illustration. They also experimented with the actual process of printing, applying the ink more or less liberally, smoothing the paper against the block with more or less pressure, and moistening the paper to different degrees. The result was a refinement of technique that allowed the engraver and printer to reproduce the same gradations in tone and shade that an artist could achieve in a brush painting—as long as that engraver and printer were highly skilled. Shen Xinyou, who published a masterpiece of color printing in *Jiezi yuan huazhuan*, the *Mustard Seed Garden Manual of Painting*, summed up the skills needed thus: if flowing line and delicate coloring were to be obtained, the engraver must be able to use a knife as if it were a brush and the printer must be able to apply tint with a broom. (The "broom" Shen refers to is the inker's brush, considerably larger and coarser than an artist's brush.)

Chinese color woodblock illustration never enjoyed the commercial viability or popularity that its Japanese counterpart did. But the technique of color woodblock printing continued to be practiced into the twentieth century and has continued into the twenty-first, in the studios of fine printers and artists, and in the workshops that produce the folk prints traditionally pasted on doors and walls at the new year.

YAQU CANGSHU, BY QIAN SHU. TWO-COLOR WOODBLOCK. PREFACE DATED 1703.

This simple example of black-and-red printing demonstrates the difference in the inks used to print from woodblocks and seals: printer's ink, whether black or polychrome, is water-based, and seal ink, oil-based. Here, the oil that has bled into the paper indicates that the seals on the illustration page were not printed by woodblock but hand-pressed.

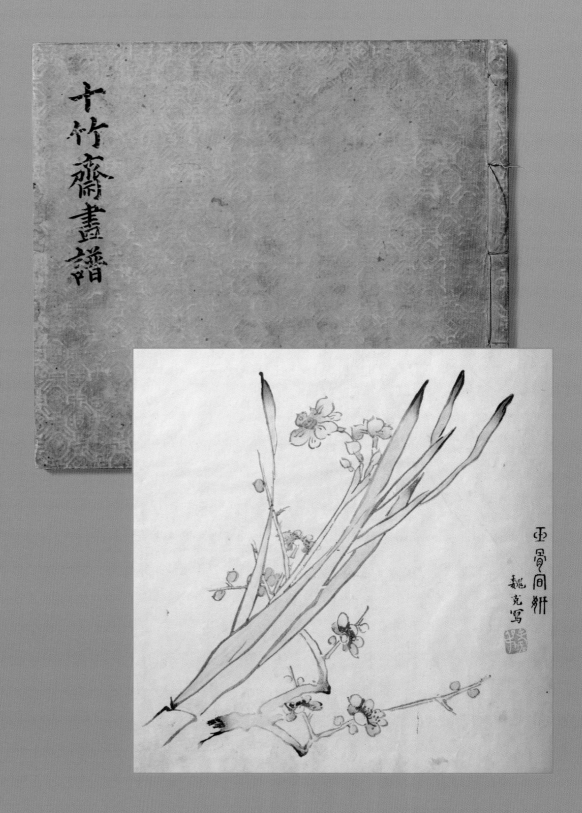

SHIZHU ZHAI SHUHUA PU, COMPILED BY HU ZHENGYAN. COLOR WOODBLOCK. 17TH CENTURY.

In China, polychrome woodblock printing was used most often in the production of painting manuals, which reproduced individual brush strokes and paintings incorporating those strokes. The first such manual printed in color, Hu Zhengyan's Ten Bamboos Studio Manual of Calligraphy and Painting, *inspired a host of imitators and admirers, the* Mustard Seed Garden Manual *among them.*

 [OPPOSITE PAGE]

JIEZI YUAN HUAZHUAN SANJI, BY WANG SHI, WANG GAI, AND WANG NIE. COLOR WOODBLOCK. 1796–1820.

Cotton rose, from the Mustard Seed Garden Manual. *Directly inspired by Hu Zhengyan's* Ten Bamboos Studio Manual, *the* Mustard Seed Garden Manual *displays a more sophisticated use of technique along with a different style of representation.*

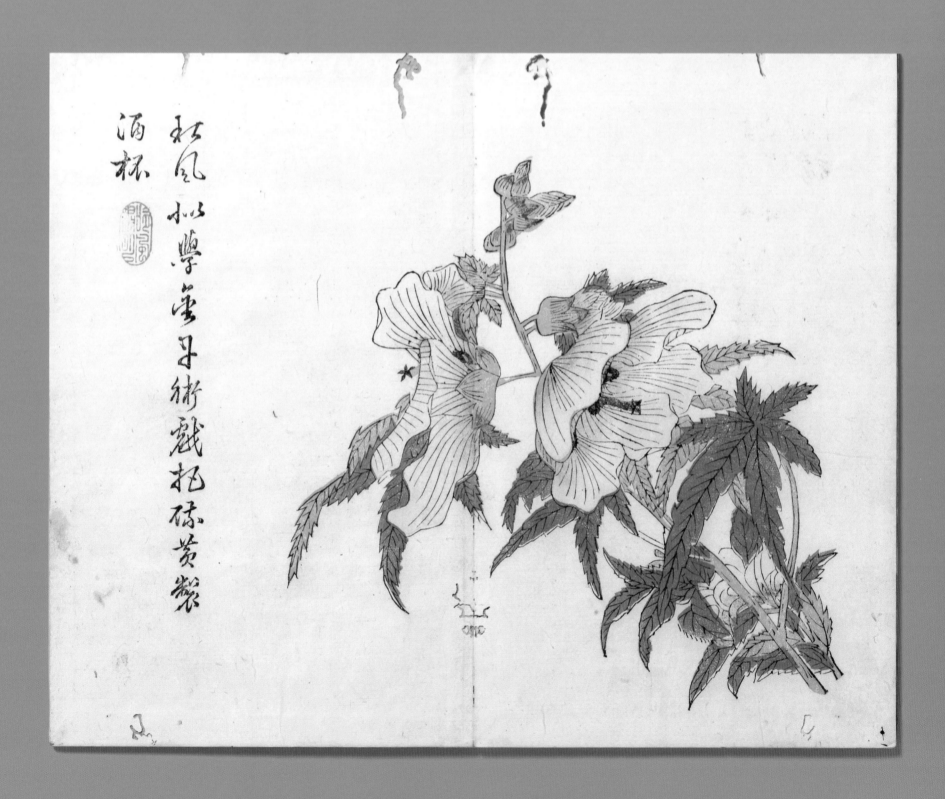

Embellishments

During Japan's fifty-year period of experimentation with movable-type printing, two men in the village of Saga, now in the northwestern quarter of Kyoto, collaborated on a number of printing projects now known as Saga-bon. Painter and calligrapher Hon'ami Kōetsu oversaw the artistic aspects of production, and the merchant Suminokura Soan managed the practical aspects.

Even among early Japanese imprints the Saga-bon were distinguished. Particular editions, called Kōetsu-bon, stand out for the sheer elegance of their design and production, with type based on Kōetsu's own running-style calligraphy and paper of various colors patterned with powdered mica. Added to ink and pressed into paper or dusted over a newly printed page, mica lends a gold or silver sheen to the paper's surface. Three hundred years after the publication of the Kōetsu-bon, artists and printers engaged by Kanao Tanejirō's press, Bun'endo, were still using the basic elements of mica, colored paper, and calligraphy in beautifully fresh variations.

Kanao Tanejirō was one of a handful of publishers in the early decades of the twentieth century engaged in the printing of "sketch tour" books devoted to landscape illustration. For the most part, these publishers employed artists highly influenced by Western technique and attitude; but they found that for the purposes of book production traditional woodblock reproduced the modernist watercolors and oils more successfully than photography and collotype. At a time when woodblock engravers were losing ground to new technologies, Kanao and his fellow publishers were seeking out skilled engravers and woodblock printers such as Nishimura Kumakichi, whose expertise could invest a block-printed illustration with the appearance of a watercolor.

The Bun'endo list carried more than landscape books and prints. Kanao was also one of the principal publishers of the poet, translator, and essayist Yosano Akiko. Like the "sketch tour" publishers, Akiko found a place for tradition in the modern world. She instilled new life in a tired poetic form, the *tanka*, and revived romanticism, pouring into her early published verse the passion and sensuality that were so conspicuously a part of her personal life.

The personal and sensual are both reflected in Bun'endo's 1918 printing of *Myōjō shō*, a collection of Akiko's short verse. The calligraphy is Akiko's own, reproduced by woodblock. The paper used is *danshi*, once favored by court ladies for their own poetry. In *Myōjō shō* the paper is printed with background designs reminiscent of the flora and architectural landmarks of Kyoto, in faint colors ranging from slate gray to coral. In the bound book, consecutive leaves never share the same pattern, and mica lightens the leaves at irregular intervals. The reference to the Kōetsu-bon is unmistakable.

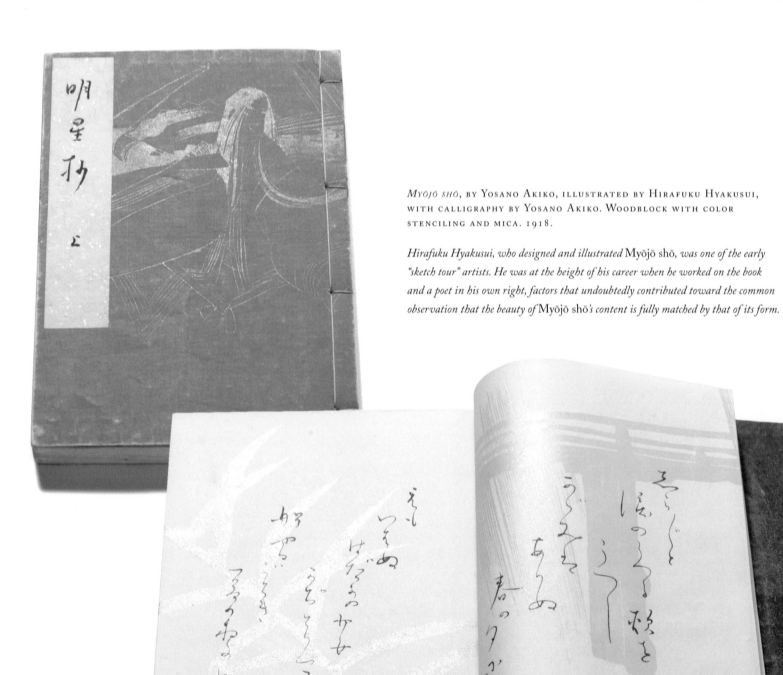

MYŌJŌ SHŌ, BY YOSANO AKIKO, ILLUSTRATED BY HIRAFUKU HYAKUSUI, WITH CALLIGRAPHY BY YOSANO AKIKO. WOODBLOCK WITH COLOR STENCILING AND MICA. 1918.

Hirafuku Hyakusui, who designed and illustrated Myōjō shō, *was one of the early "sketch tour" artists. He was at the height of his career when he worked on the book and a poet in his own right, factors that undoubtedly contributed toward the common observation that the beauty of* Myōjō shō's *content is fully matched by that of its form.*

集義堂梓行

全補故事

七寶大成

此書延吳奕齋先生所編述分類解釋
文簡而易知不惟有益於童蒙家塾老師
宿儒亦得以資其間見者其笑考其讎對
註解計三千五百餘條分為二十門題
其名曰七寶故事奕齋故可謂用心矣

Printing for a Popular Audience

Jianyang publishing

There were four great centers of printing in China during the Northern Song dynasty: Kaifeng to the north, Fuzhou to the south, Hangzhou to the east, and Chengdu to the west. Kaifeng fell to the Jurchen with the collapse of the Northern Song, and Chengdu was destroyed by Mongol invaders at the end of the Southern Song. At the start of the Ming dynasty, in the fourteenth century, much of China's printing industry was concentrated in the east and south, and much of that was concentrated at Jianyang, in what is now Fujian.

While Jianyang's publishers are known to have produced fine editions in earlier eras, by the Ming they had earned a reputation for inexpensive editions of works certain to sell—household manuals, divination texts, and fiction, among other things. As one contemporary booklover complained, these editions were printed not for the benefit of later generations, but for gain.

Even the modern reader unfamiliar with Chinese might guess on examining one of these editions that it was produced for profit. The reader might notice an obvious economy to the design and production of the book: the margins might be stingy, the number of lines per page and characters per line more than double what he would find in a fine edition, as if the engravers had taken pains to squeeze as much text as possible onto each page.

The reader might also detect a carelessness or hastiness on the part of the printers and engravers. In some places it would be apparent that too much or too little ink had been applied to the block or that it had been applied unevenly. Occasional blurred lines might suggest that one of the shop workers budged while printing off a block. Elsewhere the lack of clarity might point to other cost-cutting measures commonly practiced by commercial publishers in China—using and reusing printing blocks until they no longer produced clear images, and selling blocks or renting them out when one publisher no longer had a market for them but another had.

[PAGE 46]

XINKE LIANDUI BIAN MENG TUXIANG QIBAO GUSHI DAQUAN, BY WU DAOMING. WOODBLOCK. 1604.

This title page, in what is clearly a publisher's advertisement, boasts that the book "will benefit not only the young learner; even the teacher and seasoned scholar will increase their understanding" by reading it—and, presumably, buying it.

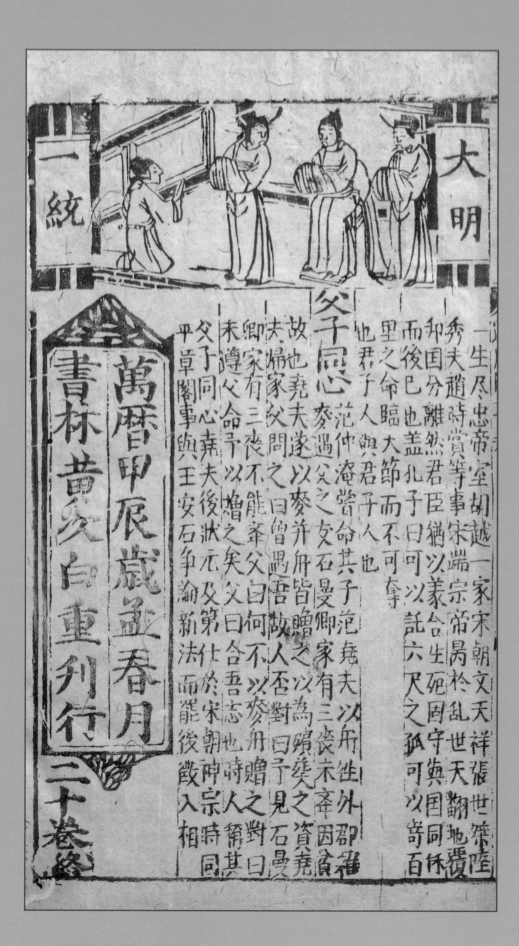

Xinke liandui bian meng tuxiang Qibao gushi daquan, by Wu Daoming. Woodblock. 1604.

This Jianyang edition names both its publisher, Huang Cibai, and his establishment, Jiyi tang. One other element in the printer's colophon points to the book's commercial nature: the colophon locates the printer's shop in the "book forest," or book quarter of the city, where commercial printers clustered.

ZHONGYI SHUIHU ZHUAN, BY SHI
NAIAN, ANNOTATED BY
LI ZHI. WOODBLOCK. 1600–1627.

*"The Murder of Ximen Qing" and "Wu
Song, Drunk, Fights Jiang Menshen."
A popular admonition warns against
allowing the young to read* Shuihu *and
the old,* Sanguo. *The fear is that that*
Sanguo, *the tale of struggle for political
and military dominance in third-century
China, will overexcite the older reader,
and that* Shuihu, Tales of the Marshes,
*recounting the exploits of a band of
renegades and fugitives, will corrupt
young minds and morals. These full-page
illustrations suggest just how the novel
lionizes the outlaws' tale in telling it.*

ILLUSTRATED POPULAR FICTION

Zheng Zhenduo, the pioneering historian of Chinese popular
literature, once noted the various characters of Chinese book
illustration. In Buddhist sutras, the illustrations are meant to
serve as devotional aids. In catalogs of archaeological artifacts
or medicinal plants, they are intended as a form of scientific
description. In painting treatises, they are included as models to
be copied and studied. In Ming anthologies of travel literature,
the woodcut landscapes and riverscapes, combining artistic
sensibility and technical expertise, possess an aesthetic value
independent of the texts they accompany.

In popular fiction and drama, the character of book illustration
was influenced by the format it followed. Illustrations in the
shangtu xiawen, "picture above, text below," format appeared on
every page, occupying roughly the top third. *Chatu*, "illustrations
inserted" into the text, were either full-page or double-page
illustrations, clustered at the beginning of a work or scattered
throughout it.

Modern scholars have suggested that the *shangtu xiawen* illustrations might have served as pictorial props for the semi-literate
reader, as pleasant diversions for the reader suffering eyestrain
brought on by poorly printed text, or as devices to drive the
narrative forward. Full-page "inserted" illustrations, in one early
commercial publisher's claim, served as supplements to understanding rather than props: "Illustrations may seem childish.
Illustrations, however, depict what words cannot....There must
be accuracy in the reproduction of scene and exactness in the
transmission of spirit." And the illustrator who succeeds in this,
the publisher states, deserves to be called, not craftsman, but
artist.

Zheng Zhenduo was more emphatic. In his estimation, illustration of popular literature, when good, reflected what the reader
encountered in the text, in both scene and spirit. The best went
further, displaying originality in execution, insight into the text,
and vigor, even after centuries on the page.

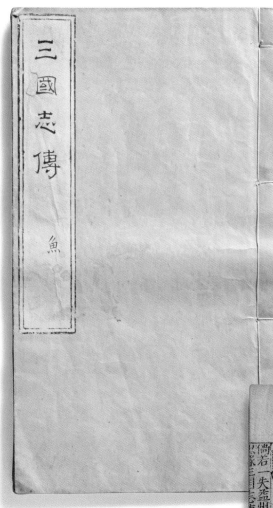

Xinqin quanxiang dazi tongsu yanyi Sanguo zhizhuan, by Luo Guanzhong. Woodblock. 1573–1644.

"*Zhang Fei Asks a Commoner the Way*" and "*The Army of Zhang He Takes Jiameng Pass.*" *This* shangtu xiawen *edition of* Sanguo *presents not the epic-length novel carefully revised by Mao Lun and Mao Zonggang but an earlier version of the tale,* The Annals of the Three Kingdoms, *in a Newly Cut, Fully Illustrated, Large-Print Edition of the Popular Tale. Whether or not the illustrations aided the reader's understanding, the title indicates that the publisher, Qiaoshan tang, of Jianyang, was confident that they would aid sales.*

SAMURAI AUTHORS

Professional writers might be hacks or stylists, intellectuals or average minds. In Tokugawa Japan, they might also be samurai. In addition to lacking profitable employment in times of peace, by the mid-seventeenth century many samurai had also lost their masters—and therefore the peacetime stipends they might have been paid—when the central government confiscated whatever fiefs it plausibly could to increase its own wealth. Some of the masterless samurai turned to farming, some found occupations in towns. Some of those sufficiently educated entered officialdom, and a prominent number wrote for commercial publication.

The audiences they targeted and the genres they wrote in varied. In the eighteenth century, Hiraga Gennai wrote a brand of fiction later tagged *kokkei-bon*, "humorous books," for the educated reader. Trained as a traditional botanist, Gennai gained exposure to Western science through the Dutch traders at Nagasaki and the community of Japanese intellectuals drawn to them. Intellectual curiosity led him voluntarily to leave his feudal lord and fixed income, to experiment with electricity and asbestos, copper and silver mining, oil painting and Dutch ceramics. He was a man of many interests and probably almost as many sources of income. He seems to have written *kokkei-bon* not for gain, however, but for the opportunity satire afforded him to criticize what he disliked in the world around him: the brothel system, Confucian learning, the hypocrisy of clerics, the craven nature of society at large. According to tradition, Gennai's publisher paid him with gifts and good times.

Half a century later, the samurai Kyokutei Bakin wrote professionally to amass a fortune by entertaining, not enlightening, his readers: "A work will always sell that is seven-tenths vulgar and three-tenths elegant," he wrote to a friend, "…one that is seven-tenths elegant and three vulgar will not sell very well,…and a work that is all elegance and not even a tenth vulgar will not sell at all." Fatherless, masterless, and penniless, Bakin had tried his hand at a number of occupations before turning to popular fiction, ultimately publishing over two hundred titles in many more volumes.

Bakin published in two formats: *yomihon*, "reading books," and *gōkan*, "collected volumes." Sparsely illustrated and literary in style, the former appealed to educated merchants and Bakin's fellow samurai. The latter, heavily illustrated, were read by a much less educated audience. Both were serial formats, which would provide steady income, given a loyal readership. Just as importantly, the tales' conventional morality and utter remove from the real world ensured that Bakin could publish without interference from the Tokugawa authorities, whose ban on pornography and works critical of the government had led to the arrest of Bakin's first mentor in the world of professional writing.

Fūryū Shidōken den, by Hiraga Gennai. Woodblock. 1763.

Like Swift's Gulliver's Travels, *Gennai's* Elegant Tale of Shidōken, *published under the pseudonym Fūrai Sanjin, dresses criticism of the current world in the guise of an imaginary travel narrative. The tale is told by Shidōken himself, here pictured with the fan that allowed him to fly through the air and sail over water, and the wooden baton with which, as a storyteller, he punctuated his performances— funny enough, according to the opening chapter, to make the listener shake his navel loose laughing.*

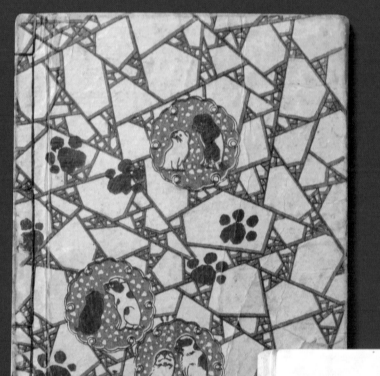

NANSŌ SATOMI HAKKENDEN, BY KYOKUTEI BAKIN, ILLUSTRATED BY
YANAGAWA SHIGENOBU. WOODBLOCK. 1823.

*Bakin specialized in historical narratives that were accurate in detail, didactic
in tone, fantastic in plot and storyline. Here, a double-page illustration from his
immensely successful* yomihon *titled* Tale of the Eight Dogs of Satomi of Nansō,
initially published in 106 volumes between 1814 and 1842.

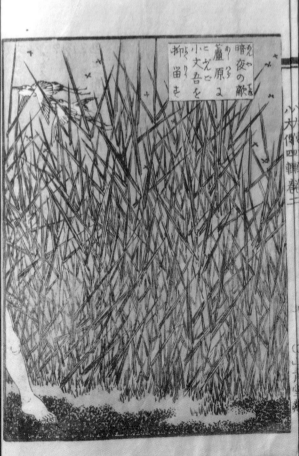

Pulp fiction

Before there were *manga*, there were *kusazōshi*, popular publications that targeted less educated readers and consequently laid as much emphasis on illustration as on text, if not more. In the seventeenth and eighteenth centuries, *akahon*, or red-covered books, were devoted to children's stories. *Kurohon*, with black covers, and *aohon*, with blue, recounted folktales, stories from history, and the plots of popular drama for an older audience. *Kibyoshi*, with yellow jackets, frequently satirized the present by pretending to relate tales set in the past and aimed at juvenile readers. When the shogunate made its disapproval of the veiled criticism felt, the humor quickly faded and children once again became the *kibyoshi*'s actual intended audience.

A new subgenre of *kusazōshi* appeared toward the beginning of the nineteenth century, *gōkan*, or "collected volumes." *Gōkan* differed from earlier types of *kusazōshi* most noticeably in their extravagantly colored covers. They were published serially for reasons of economy: titles that didn't sell well could be terminated quickly, titles that proved popular could be extended, and the process of printing and publishing could begin before the writing was completed. Individual volumes were thin and were usually sewn together, as the name suggests, into booklets of anywhere from two to ten volumes. The total number of volumes making up a title could reach as many as ninety.

Early *gōkan* focused on tales of vengeance or historical themes; later titles expanded into romance and stories from the Kabuki theatre. The author of *Rustic Genji*, Ryūtei Tanehiko, managed to offer a bit of each in his serial based loosely on the eleventh-century *Tale of Genji*, relocated to the pleasure quarters and the days of the Ashikaga shogunate. Tanehiko brought out the first installment of his *gōkan* in 1829, unsure of how it would be received. Immensely popular, *Rustic Genji* continued publication for the next twelve years. It is said that when illness delayed the appearance of one new volume, a lady of the shogun's court made repeated temple visits for the sake of Tanehiko's recovery and that many others joined her in prayer.

[OPPOSITE PAGE]

Nise Murasaki inaka Genji, by Ryūtei Tanehiko, illustrated by Utagawa Kunisada. Color woodblock. 1833.

A fellow samurai and rival of Bakin's in the world of commercial fiction, Ryūtei Tanehiko first tried his hand at yomihon *before finding success with* gōkan. *Unlike Bakin, Tanehiko attracted the interest of the Tokugawa authorities, who charged him with corrupting public morals just as printing blocks for the last two installments of* Rustic Genji *were being carved. The blocks were destroyed and the author arrested. The missing installments were eventually printed in the twentieth century.*

Zatsudan amayo no shichigura, by Tamenaga Shunsui,
illustrated by Kunihisa. Woodblock. 1857–61.

The kusazōshi's *printed page characteristically presents an integration of picture
and text. Cursive script appears wherever the illustration allows; printer's devices
may guide the reader from one passage of text to the next; figures in the stories are
identified by an abbreviated form of their name, often in a circular cartouche placed
somewhere on their robes.*

Korō monogatari, text and illustrations by Torii Kiyostune. Woodblock. Undated.

While ukiyo-e *artists were commissioned for later* kibyoshi *and* gōkan *authored by professional writers, earlier* kusazōshi *were often illustrated and written by a single person. Many artists of the Torii school, including Kiyotsune, produced* kurohon *and* aohon.

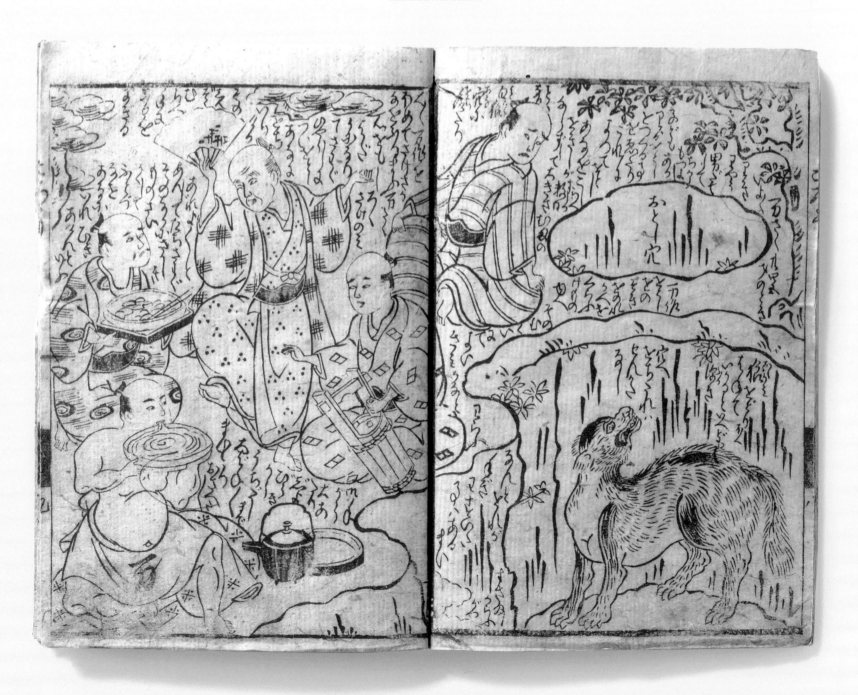

Kuchi-e

When Japanese printers experimented with movable type in the early seventeenth century, they found that they could adapt the technology to satisfy aesthetic standards but not market forces. They consequently abandoned the new technology after a period of fifty years. By the time the Dutch reintroduced movable type in the mid-nineteenth century, conditions had changed: urban populations had increased in absolute numbers and in relative rates of literacy. Movable type found a place in printing and publishing, and within another fifty years it was woodblock technology that had become economically unviable.

Unviable, that is, only as a cheap means of printing text on a large scale. The woodblock, especially the color woodblock, retained its aesthetic appeal in the realm of illustration even while lithography, photography, and copperplate engraving were gaining wider use. Between 1890 and 1912, publishers found that color woodblock frontispieces, or *kuchi-e*, could be successful selling points for new fiction, and they commissioned skilled artists, engravers, and printers in need of work to produce them.

Generally, *kuchi-e* printing blocks were prepared and printed from just as *ukiyo-e* blocks were. Occasionally fine touches were added—powdered mica, burnished black ink, or *bokashi*, the gradation of color obtained by judicious application of water to the block at the time of printing. Some prints fit snugly onto a small page, but most were larger, requiring folding into halves or thirds. Some were tipped in, others sewn in, mounted or unmounted. Frequently the artist's, and sometimes the engraver's or printer's, name or seal appears carved into the block.

Gotō Chūkai, a novelist active during the Meiji era, argued that publishers should not include *kuchi-e* in newly published novels. The beauty of the prints was at odds with the cheap typeset editions they occurred in, and they raised the price of a book—the cost of producing a single *kuchi-e* could equal all other publication costs combined. But he knew that publishers would continue to include *kuchi-e* as long as the frontispieces attracted buyers that the author or title alone could not.

Konjiki yasha, by Ozaki Kōyō, frontispiece by Takeuchi Keishū. Color woodblock frontispiece. 1898.

This kuchi-e *from* The Gold Demon *took on iconic status shortly after it appeared on bookstore shelves. First serialized in the newspaper* Yomiuri shimbun, *the novel tells the story of a student whose fiancée breaks off their engagement to marry a wealthy suitor. The student rebuffs his former fiancée in this well-known scene. The* kuchi-e *was popularly interpreted as a criticism of modernization and the wholesale adoption of Western values. Atami, where the scene is set, annually honors the author of the novel, Ozaki Kōyō, and the site itself has become a regular tourist stop.*

FUTARI MINASHIGO, BY TENGAI, FRONTISPIECE BY KAJITA HANKO.
COLOR WOODBLOCK FRONTISPIECE. 1903.

With the demise of the feudal system in 1868, many artists lost the wealthy patrons who had supported them. Like so many other kuchi-e *illustrators, Kajita Hanko, whose printed signature appears in the lower right corner of this* kuchi-e, *received formal training in painting but turned to newspaper and book illustration in order to earn a living. Unlike other illustrators, he received recognition for his painting. He also observed a theoretical distinction between illustrations, which he believed should serve as reading aids, and* kuchi-e, *which he felt should have an appeal and aesthetic interest independent of the underlying novel.*

SENKEN NAGAYA, BY SHIMAMURA HŌGETSU, FRONTISPIECE BY
KABURAKI KIYOKATA. COLOR WOODBLOCK FRONTISPIECE. 1908.

Publishers' announcements not only advertised the inclusion of kuchi-e *but often
gave equal prominence to artists' and authors' names. Some even noted whether the*
kuchi-e *were block-printed or lithographed. The verso of this unmounted* kuchi-e
*indicates that it was block-printed by hand: the faint streaking is evidence of the
printer's* baren, *the pad used to press dampened paper laid over the inked woodblock.*

破滿慈執相
難性顯如來藏
初答藏性生相
次答大性俱徧
後次一釋滿慈
本疑次釋度

大佛頂首楞嚴經疏解蒙鈔卷四之一

海印弟子蒙叟錢謙益鈔

長水判經第一大科顯如來藏心之二從此下盡
本卷中如何自欺尚留視聽今謹益判經從此去
逕卷六卷文殊説圓竟為經次分之一
躡上題如來藏心大科破滿慈執相難性顯如來
藏為大文下之第二大科次下以致請詳宣答釋三
科為承起科以初答藏性生相次答大性俱徧為大
科下第一子科藏性科中以一正答所疑二別答盡妨為第
二子科初中又以初破滿慈能所執見次正顯迷
真起妄之由為重起母科[redacted]又以通明妄覺於
真之相廣雜二相是轉生由為重起子科㊂又以一
立因相二雜果相為別起母科以下因明三相果
有即性即相名第一義是佛所證決定無妄審實名
諦二引經世尊常推説法人中我為第一富樓那
述迷迷

智論二

Transmission of Texts

Banned Books

In early and medieval China, censorship was imposed to protect orthodox thought. At the outset of the Qin dynasty, for example, the First Emperor ordered the burning of all books except those of the most practical value—works on agriculture, medicine, and divination—and during the Tang dynasty, the statesman and literatus Han Yu called for the burning of all Buddhist works.

In later ages censorship was also used to punish individuals who spoke out against powerful ministers or the throne itself. During the Qianlong reign of the Manchu Qing dynasty, such sedition was hunted out with particular zeal. As the case of Qian Qianyi demonstrates, it was not necessary that the condemned work contain sensitive material or that it be current in order to incur imperial censure.

Qian Qianyi is best remembered today for his contributions to the study of Chinese poetry, his marriage to the courtesan Liu Rushi, and his controversial politics. An official under the Ming dynasty, he accepted office under the Manchus after their conquest of China, a concession that was common at the time but still morally questionable. After accepting office, however, he maintained contact with Ming loyalists, an association that made him suspect in his new masters' eyes. He eventually fell into disfavor with the court, which imposed a ban on Qian's work in the last years of his life.

In 1769, over a hundred years after Qian's death, the Qianlong emperor found Qian's writings to be "an insult to right doctrines" and decreed that they be eradicated from the corpus of Chinese literature. All bookstores and private collectors were to submit their copies of Qian's books to the local yamen for burning; all woodblocks used to print them were to be sent to the imperial capital. Provincial governors were to see to it that news of the decree reached even the remotest areas of the empire. Subsequent decrees called for Qian's verse and prose, and even his name, to be excised from collective works and gazetteers, and cut out of the printing blocks that had produced them. Nothing of Qian's thought was to be left to posterity.

As harsh and as thoroughgoing as the literary inquisition of Qianlong was, it ended abruptly with the emperor's death, in 1795, and by the end of the nineteenth century, Qian's works were being reprinted in China. They had survived in Japan; some had survived in China as well, possibly in the libraries of Manchu collectors, who were quietly exempted from responding to the purges. Scholars have speculated that a member of the Manchu imperial house who owned a portion of Qian's personal library, Prince Yi, might have been responsible for preserving some of Qian's works. Prince Yi's library was dispersed in 1861 when the male descendant who had inherited it became embroiled in a failed coup.

[PAGE 64]

DAFODING SHOULENGYAN JING SHUJIE MENGCHAO, ANNOTATED BY QIAN QIANYI. MANUSCRIPT, IN QIAN'S HAND. CA. 1660.

In 1660 Qian published an annotated recension of the Śūrangamasutra, *but his fall from favor disrupted the book's publication and distribution; as a result, copies of the original edition are rare. Incredibly, the complete draft manuscript resurfaced in the antiquarian book market in the 1920s. Only four volumes of the original ten are known of today. The volume pictured here was once in the Miyun lou, the library of the collector Chiang Meng-p'ing. Qian's seal appears at the bottom right.*

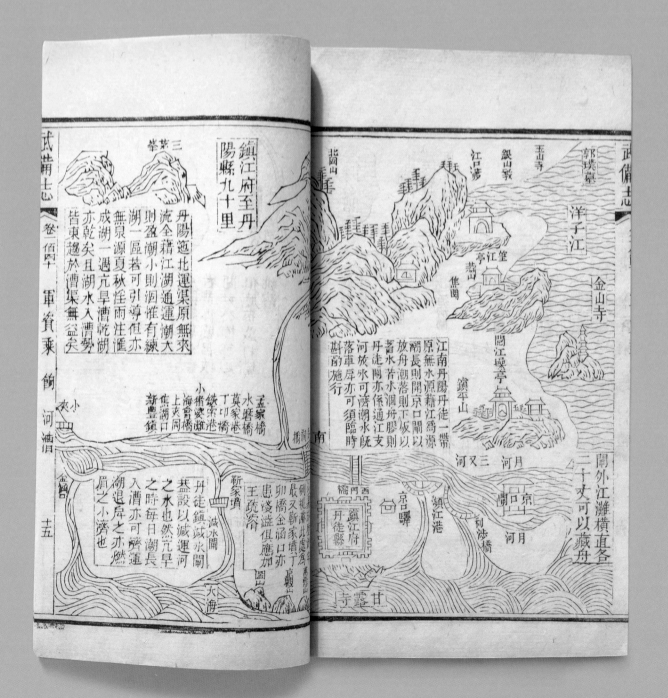

WUBEI ZHI, BY MAO YUANYI. WOODBLOCK. 1621.

It has been estimated that over twenty-six hundred works, from all fields of study and literary genres, were enrolled on the emperor's Index expurgatorius. *Most were deemed to contain instances of lèse-majesté or information critical to national security. When Mao Yuanyi first presented his* Treatise on Military Preparations *to the Ming throne in 1621, his chief concern was the threat posed by the Manchus to the north. After the Manchu conquest of China, the treatise was placed on the emperor's index purportedly because of the aid it might render potential insurrectionists.*

Unpublishable material

In 1744, at the age of nine, the girl who would become Lady Hyegyŏng entered the palace at Seoul to marry the crown prince, Sado, himself still a boy. In 1762, she was widowed when Sado's father, King Yŏngjo, ordered him into a rice chest and had it sealed, causing his son to suffocate. By some accounts, Sado was insane and rightly punished for criminal acts committed; by others, he was the victim of factional struggles at court.

Sado's son ruled as king from the death of Yŏngjo, in 1776, until his own death, in 1800. By then, Lady Hyegyŏng had already written one memoir, which focused on her paternal family and was commonly regarded as a justification for her and her father's decision not to commit suicide at Sado's death. After Lady Hyegyŏng's grandson ascended the throne, she wrote further memoirs: the second is considered a defense of a brother and a paternal uncle, executed for conversion to Catholicism and sedition, respectively; the third recalls the ways in which her son, Chŏngjo, sought to rehabilitate the memory of his father, and repeats the author's desire to see the same done for her uncle and brother; the fourth recounts the events leading up to Yŏngjo's ordering Sado into the rice chest.

Lady Hyegyŏng's memoirs opposed both literary tradition and palace convention. There was no established genre of women's autobiographical writing; even if there had been, court custom would have forbidden the airing of so horrendous an episode as Sado's death. Lady Hyegyŏng addressed the memoirs to male relatives—the first to her nephew, and the second, third, and fourth to her grandson, King Sunjo—and apparently entrusted the original manuscripts to the persons addressed. The author did not write the memoirs to be published, nor would they have been publishable.

Manuscript copies of the original memoirs were made, but they remained in the circle of the royal family, coming to public attention only in 1939, when portions of one were published in a literary magazine. Since then, scholars have tracked down fourteen manuscript copies, have studied, transcribed, annotated, translated, and published them. The memoirs became a popular success in Korea, in part because of the strange story they tell, in part because of Lady Hyegyŏng's extraordinary rendering of the tale, in a voice at once restrained and impassioned, delicate yet candid, informed but ready to acknowledge that some matters are not easily understood.

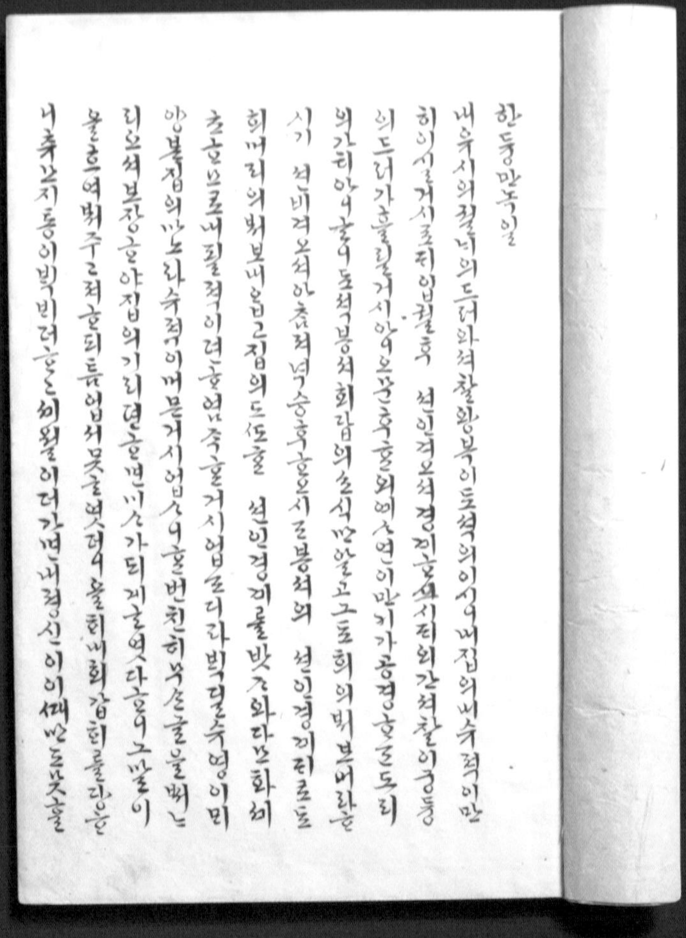

Hanjungnok, by Hyegyŏnggung Hong Ssi. Manuscript. Undated.

Copies of the memoirs written in han'gŭl, *like the one pictured here, would have been intended for female readers within the royal circle, who would not have been taught to read or write in classical Chinese. The few Chinese or Chinese-* han'gŭl *manuscripts that have been found are believed to have been translated from the* han'gŭl *originals for the benefit of male readers.*

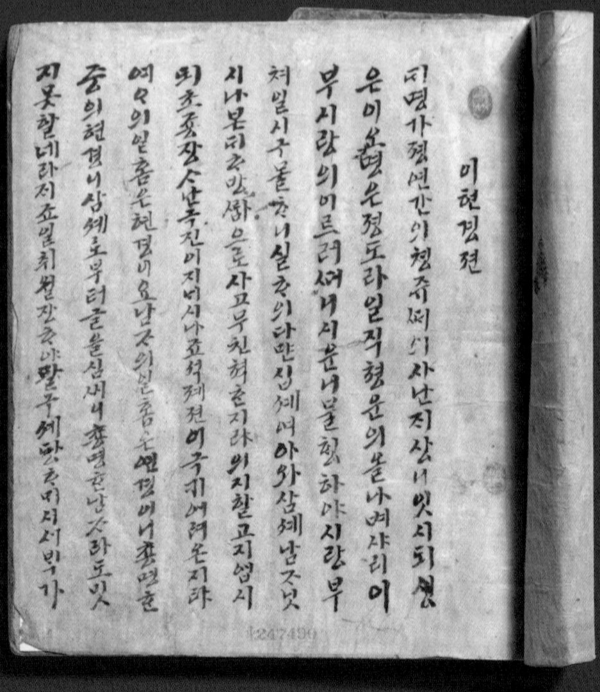

Yi Hyŏn-gyŏng chŏn. Manuscript. 1912.

The central government's strict insistence on orthodox thought and the dampening influence it exercised over commercial publishing began to relax toward the end of the dynastic era, and women began to write for public consumption. Today, domestic novels like The Story of Yi Hyŏn-gyŏng, *novels that did not make it to press but circulated in manuscript, are being rediscovered and published for the first time, if not on their literary merits, then on the basis of their interest to social and cultural historians.*

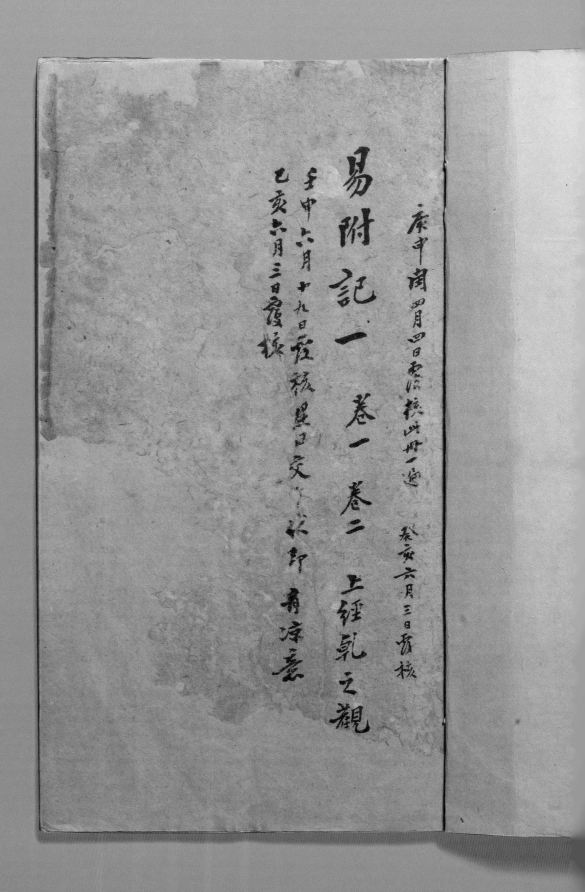

Yi fu ji, by Weng Fanggang.
Manuscript, in Weng's hand.
Ca. 1800.

*In the draft preface to his commentary to
the* Book of Songs, *Weng mentions that
he had been collecting material for the work
over a number of years. On the covers of
his commentary to the* Book of Changes,
*Weng records the dates he reviewed the
manuscript—in all, three times over a
space of fifteen years.*

MANUSCRIPTS

Manuscripts inform in different ways. The handwriting may suggest the author's character or emotional state at writing. Corrections may offer insight into the author's thoughts or writing method. The substance of a manuscript never intended for publication can give later readers a fresh view of a public event or historical era. Draft manuscripts of works written for publication but never printed can also reveal much about their authors, even when those authors are well published.

Weng Fanggang was a leading scholar of the mid-Qing dynasty. He served in a number of official capacities, including editor of the collectanea *Siku quanshu, All Writings in the Four Treasuries*, where he was charged with selecting or arriving at authoritative editions of works to be reprinted in the collection. In his late sixties Weng took up an honorary post that gave him the time to write a series of commentaries on the Confucian classics. According to his diary, he had completed twelve such commentaries by 1804, fourteen years before his death; only four, however, were ever published.

Original manuscripts of four of the missing commentaries have recently come to light. One modern scholar who reviewed them has found in them language expressing at times scholarly frustration, at times actual hostility, toward contemporary senior scholars, sentiments found only in a draft manuscript of Weng's miscellaneous writings and nowhere in writings published during his lifetime. The revelation is significant from more than a gossipmonger's point of view. Weng had a reputation during his lifetime and after for mediating between two contentious schools of classical studies. The manuscripts suggest that he spent a good deal of effort and patience to maintain that stance.

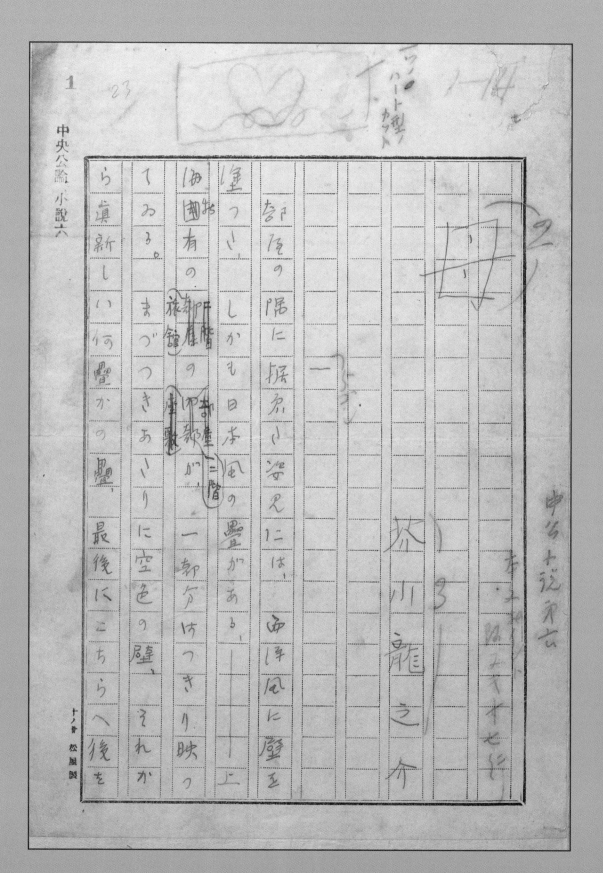

"HAHA," BY AKUTAGAWA RYŪNOSUKE. MANUSCRIPT, IN AKUTAGAWA'S HAND. 1921.

The original manuscript of "Mothers," by Akutagawa Ryūnosuke, author of "In a Grove," the short story that director Kurosawa Akira worked into film as Rashomon. This manuscript was written at a pivotal time in Akutagawa's life, at the onset of the physical and nervous disorders that would end only with his suicide six years later. Some will read in his hand a nervousness that naturally is not present in any typeset version of the story.

Inhang ilgi. Manuscript. Ca. 1888.

In an attempt to avert Japanese aggression, Korea entered a series of commercial treaties with Western powers in the 1880s. The first to be concluded was the treaty with the United States, negotiated at Inchon in 1882 by Admiral R. W. Schufeldt and Korean emissaries Sin Hŏn and Kim Hong-jip, with the aid of Chinese representatives Ma Jianzhong and Ding Ruchang. This diary, kept by an unnamed member of Sin Hŏn's staff, includes, among other things, details concerning changes in the treaty's wording.

率隨員四人及天津水師總教習英國人一

今月初一日午時量請國使臣丁汝昌馬建忠

啓本

期在朝鮮下付標指定何處四字

跋尾同在朝鮮下仁川府三字添入　一年爲

原文稍覽體面

頭付筆話此一款專指美商在貴國而言較

條　方准同需下專條二字抹去

条改以美國官民必將互訂酬報之專

立有專條　彼此須照酬報互訂之專

惟於優待他國利益係出於甘壞立有

字

第十四款朝鮮二字改爲大朝鮮國王五

運出十三字添入

第八款遵辦下惟仁川一口米粮一槪不准

二字添入

第六款買屋居改以買地應管高民下賤產

第四款折毀改以搶封燒毀業魁改以罪犯

第二款總領事改以領事

Kurofune raikō Uraga okatame no zu. Ink and color on paper. Ca. 1853.

The author of this manuscript witnessed less diplomatic negotiations—the arrival of the American "black ships" under the command of Commodore Matthew Perry. Perry sailed into Tokyo Bay on the morning of July 8, 1853, anchoring off Uraga; on the morning of July 14, Perry landed at Kurihama to meet with Japanese officials. The intimidating sight of the ships is thought to have contributed to the conclusion of the Treaty of Shimoda the following year, opening Japanese ports to American ships and Japanese waters to American whalers. The large ship here is the steam frigate Susquehanna, *flagship of the July 1853 mission.*

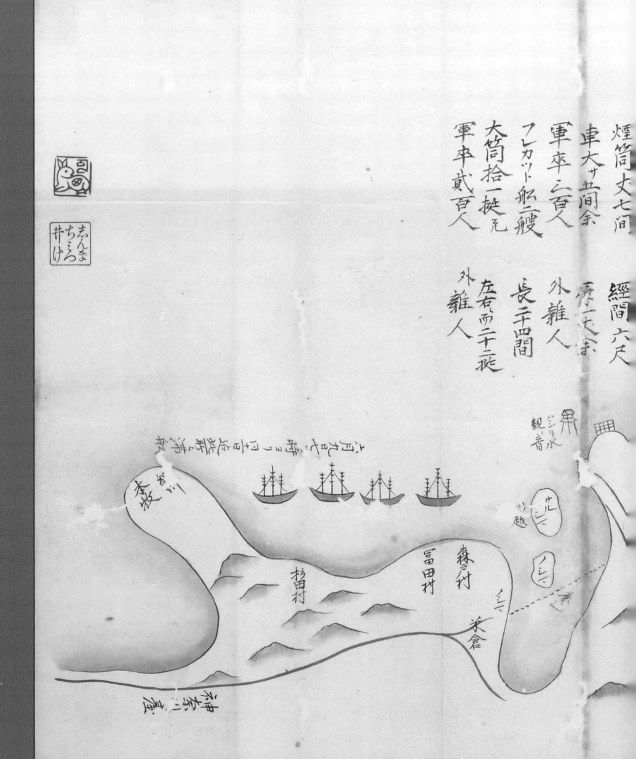

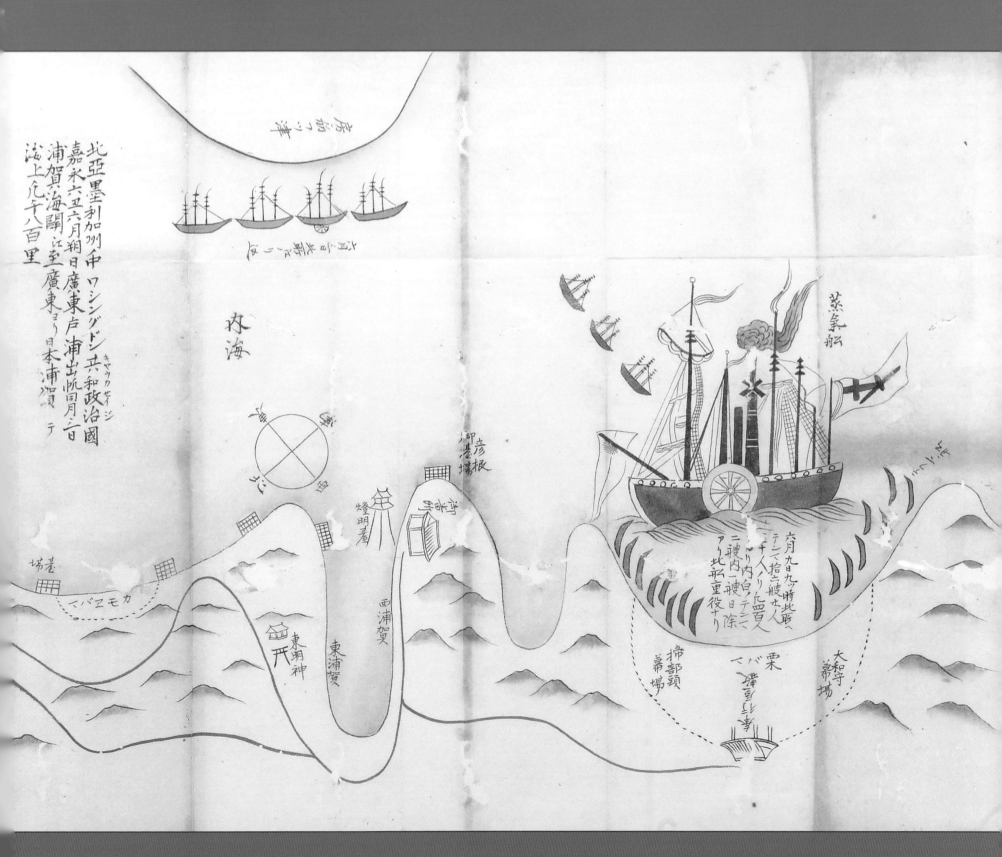

Personal copies

Even after the official, private, and commercial introduction of printing, it was not uncommon for Chinese scholars and bibliophiles to copy out books, or portions of books, by hand. Most often this occurred when the collector encountered a seldom-seen text or perhaps a volume that was missing from a broken set in his own library. Occasionally books circulated for centuries in manuscript copy only. *Xiqing shihua*, a collection of anecdotes about poets written by the Northern Song scholar-official Cai Tao, is a work of this sort.

Cai Tao lived in a time of turbulent politics. Outside its borders, non-Chinese tribes threatened China's sovereignty; inside, a host of domestic issues threatened the throne. The empire's minister, Wang Anshi, was bent on implementing a program of reforms; in opposition was a group who believed the measures ill conceived. Incapable of compromise and intolerant of opposition, Wang had his opponents cashiered, replacing them with officials outwardly of a mind with him but thoroughly corrupt. Chief among them was Cai Tao's father, Cai Jing. Succeeding Wang Anshi as minister, Cai Jing granted his son the authority of office without the formality of appointment, incidentally presenting him an opportunity to practice graft on the same scale he himself had. Father and son were eventually dismissed from office and banished from the capital. A year later the dynasty fell to Jurchen invaders.

Some literary historians have suggested that Cai Tao's sudden dismissal and the chaos of the Jurchen conquest kept Cai from finishing or publishing his *Xiqing shihua*. Others have questioned whether Cai really could have been the author of the work, since much of it is given over to vignettes concerning men his father had helped ruin. Historical rumor has claimed that Cai Tao's secretary actually authored the work; that Cai Tao wrote the work as a means of keeping track of his father's political opponents; and, unconvincingly, that Cai Tao was actually sympathetic to the cashiered statesmen.

In spite of the curious nature of its authorship, the text's authenticity has never been doubted. It is documented in private collectors' catalogs dating to the Southern Song, and a truncated version was printed in the fourteenth-century collectanea *Shuofu*. Most of the Ming manuscript copies recorded in Qing collectors' catalogs have not survived to the present day. One copy that has was recently published in a typeset edition, putting the full text of *Xiqing shihua* into print for the first time in almost a millennium.

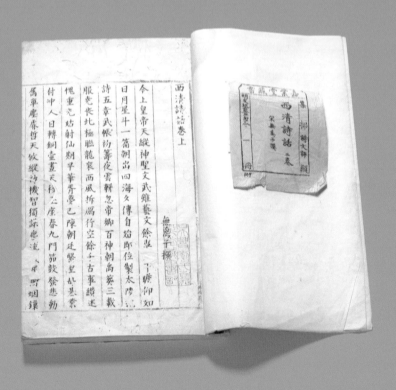

Xiqing shihua, ATTRIBUTED
TO CAI TAO. MANUSCRIPT.
MING DYNASTY.

Although many manuscript copies of
Xiqing shihua, *including this one,*
have named Anonymous as author,
the attribution to Cai Tao is the most
commonly accepted attribution, if not
an undisputed one.

CHUJŎNG. MANUSCRIPT. UNDATED.

Not all hand copies were made by
serious collectors. Enthusiastic readers
frequently wrote out quotations from
different texts pertaining to a particular
subject, creating their own commonplace
books. This commonplace book, obviously
added to over the years, collects passages
concerning wine.

YŪHAI, COMPILED BY WANG
YINGLIN. WOODBLOCK. 1340.

*The block from which this page was
printed was clearly in need of recarving.
Some of the characters have virtually
disappeared with wear, and a crack has
asserted itself through the middle of the
printing block. The lines marking the
columns of text, the* jie, *have been redrawn
with brush and ink. The printing dates
to the Ming.*

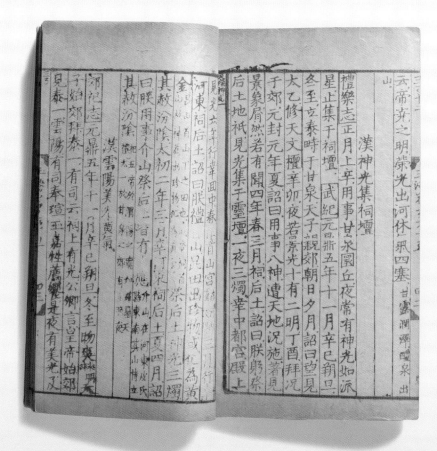

WUDAI SHI QUEWEN, BY WANG
YUCHENG. MANUSCRIPT, IN
PENG YUANRUI'S HAND. 1787.

*The Qing dynasty official Peng Yuanrui
took advantage of his position on the
editorial board of the* Siku quanshu *to
borrow a volume of* Passages Missing
from the History of the Five Dynasties
*for hand-copying. In marginalia opposite
the opening page, Peng complains of
finding printer's errors in the borrowed
copy as well as in other print editions
of the work.*

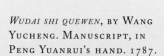

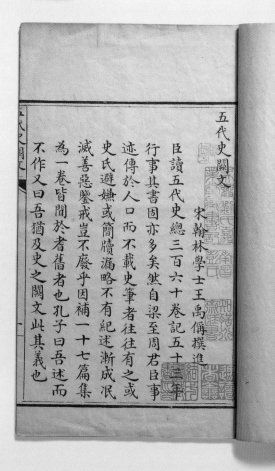

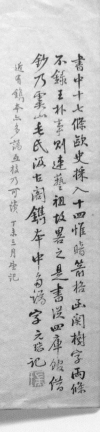

ERROR IN TRANSMISSION

In the days of the Western letterpress, the proposition of letting lead type stand in the forms in which it had been set represented an investment that was not earning a return. As soon as demand for a book was exhausted, printers consequently distributed standing type to make it available for other jobs. In traditional China, the engraving of woodblocks required a much smaller capital outlay, material and labor being both plentiful and cheap. And since the blocks, once carved, generally could not be recarved for use on other jobs, after the initial printing they were stored for future use. In the premodern Chinese book market, it was more economical to issue a new printing of even a few dozen copies of a book than to keep large quantities of stock sitting on shelves until it sold.

As relatively inexpensive as they were, blocks were not discarded and replaced once they were worn, slightly damaged, or found to contain an error. They could be touched up or repaired; plugs could be inserted to amend text. Some blocks continued to be printed from in this way for centuries.

In spite of their durability, blocks were not invulnerable to deterioration, nor were they proof against the insertion of textual errors. The Yuan engraving of the Song dynasty encyclopedia *Yuhai, Jade Sea*, provides a good example. The work of engraving was completed in 1352. In the early decades of the sixteenth century it was reported that of the five thousand blocks required to print the book, 435 were in need of replacement. Over the following decades and centuries, repairs were made to the blocks repeatedly and thousands of replacement blocks were carved, reportedly because of wear, decay, and insect damage. One modern scholar has suggested that the blocks suffered especially during the juncture between the Ming and Qing dynasties, when the storehouse in which the blocks sat remained locked and unvisited. By 1738, virtually none of the original Yuan blocks remained in the set, having all been replaced. In 1805 the storehouse caught fire and the replacement blocks burned.

After the fire of 1805, a provincial official undertook the task of having a new set of blocks carved. Regrettably, he chose to use as his base text a printing dating to the late sixteenth or early seventeenth century that was already lacking leaves. Roughly a century later, a commercial publisher decided to issue a new edition of *Jade Sea*. Conscious of the degree of deviation that had crept into the text over the centuries, he collated the nineteenth-century printing against a Yuan printing from the original blocks. Valued for its age and rarity, the Yuan printing had also come to be valued for its textual authority even though *Jade Sea* had been intermittently in print for over half a millennium.

PART II—*Cultural Impressions*

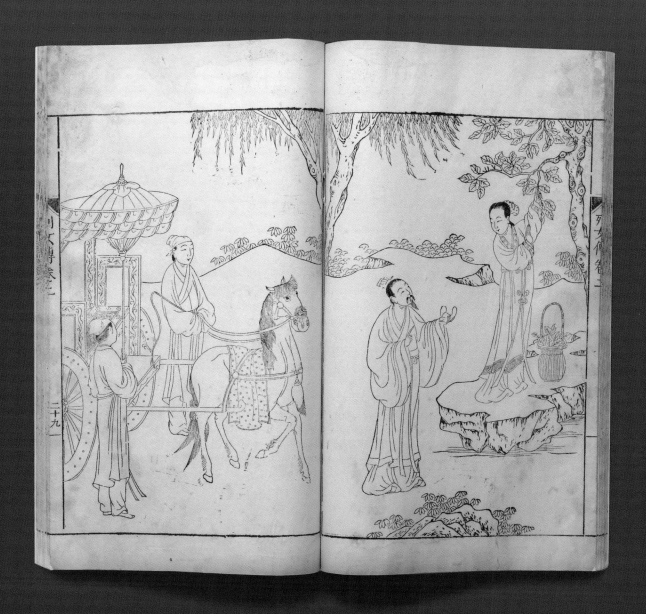

LIENÜ ZHUAN, BY LIU XIANG, EDITED BY WANG DAOKUN, ILLUSTRATIONS ATTRIBUTED TO QIU YING. WOODBLOCK. 1779.

Returning home after years of service abroad, Qiu Huzi tried to seduce an attractive woman by the side of the road, offering her the gold he was bringing to his widowed mother. He later learned that the woman was his wife. She upbraided him for his lasciviousness but more particularly for his lack of concern for his mother. "If you cannot serve your parent with filiality," she admonished, "you cannot serve your lord with loyalty." Finding the thought of life with such a man as abhorrent as the thought of taking a second husband, the Chaste Wife of Qiu Huzi drowned herself.

The Three Teachings

Confucian Morality

In the eighteenth-century novel of manners *Dream of the Red Chamber*, the young widow Li Wan is portrayed as a paragon of feminine Confucian virtue, a role for which she had been bred and educated. When she was a girl, her father had strictly limited her reading to *Nü sishu*, the *Four Books of the Women's Canon*, and *Lienü zhuan, Biographies of Eminent Women*.

Lienü zhuan was compiled just before the beginning of the Christian era, during the late Western Han, when the misplaced loyalties of imperial consorts and the rapaciousness of their families had weakened the dynasty to the point of collapse. Observing this and hoping to instruct the Son of Heaven in what was to be expected of court women, the scholar-official Liu Xiang combed the canonical literature for exemplars of female virtue and vice and collected them in the *Biographies*. One eleventh-century editor identified the virtues as motherly devotion, worthiness, prudence, compliance, integrity, and moral persuasiveness; the vice was depravity. While Liu Xiang's effort failed to save the Western Han, which fell a quarter century after his death, he did succeed in establishing an ideal, albeit an impossible ideal, for female moral deportment and decorum for centuries to come.

Toward the end of the sixteenth century, during the Ming dynasty, the scholar-official Lü Kun, inspired by the *Biographies*, compiled a similar collection, his *Gui fan*, or *Standards for the Women's*

GUI FAN, BY LÜ KUN, ILLUSTRATED BY HUANG YINGCHUN. WOOD-BLOCK. 1590–1620.

Wangsun Gu was fifteen years old and in the service of King Min of Qi when the king was assassinated. Rather than attempt to shield her son from harm, Wangsun Gu's mother urged him to continue to serve his lord. On that, the boy raised a militia, which hunted down the would-be usurper and allowed order to be restored. Lü Kun's commentary points out that a woman of tenderer feelings would have protected her son but failed to instill in him a sense of righteousness.

Quarters. The Ming is famous for government recognition of virtuous women, chaste widows in particular. Lü Kun nonetheless saw little to praise in the prevailing ways of his age. In his preface to the *Standards*, Lü complained that the ethical training of privileged and common women alike had been ignored. This was in part because the ancient texts traditionally used for moral instruction were difficult to read, their lessons veiled, their organization haphazard, their appeal dim. Lü's collection, therefore, was organized clearly and glossed where necessary. Each section was prefaced with an elucidating essay, and each tale concluded by an edifying encomium.

Lü's text was also illustrated, both to lend the work interest and to aid in impressing its lessons on the reader's mind. The author of one forward to the work, Wu Yunqing, wrote that the illustrations were intended both to please and to enlighten: "No one could ever tire of following the examples portrayed in them." Wu noted that the illustrations were included in emulation of earlier works, the *Biographies* among them.

Unlike Liu Xiang, Lü had not intended his text for the imperial court. One of the Wanli emperor's favorites, the Precious Consort Zheng, admired the book just the same, without, unfortunately, taking its lessons to heart. She financed a new printing of the *Standards* supplemented by a preface bearing her name and professing her concern for the empire's subjects, an act many viewed as disingenuous: her sentiments were appropriate for the mother of the future emperor but not the mother of a princeling, and Consort Zheng had been scheming to have her own son named heir to the throne, over the heir apparent. Lü himself was accused of abetting the Consort, thwarted in his career when he denounced her, and suspected by the imperial court when an anonymously published pamphlet critical of the Consort's ambition appeared.

In spite of the unethical behavior associated with the early history of the *Standards*, the text itself enjoyed continued popularity well into the Qing dynasty—even as certain members of the intelligentsia, such as the author of *Dream of the Red Chamber*, were questioning the wisdom of circumscribing the education of women.

TEIKAN ZUSETSU, BY ZHANG JUZHENG AND LÜ DIAOYANG. WOODBLOCK. 1650.

Emperors could also serve as moral exemplars, for both commoner and court. After the draft of Dijian tushuo, *Illustrated Discourses on the Mirror of the Emperors, was presented to the Ming throne, deluxe editions were produced for members of the elite and less refined editions for less elevated audiences. This edition was produced for the Japanese book-buying public. Here, an illustration of imperial behavior not to be emulated: the First Emperor's assignment of an expedition to seek the elusive isles of immortality, believed located in the seas east of China.*

IPHAK TOSŎL, BY KWŎN KŬN.
WOODBLOCK. 1547.

*"Heaven and Man, Mind and Nature,
Are One." Kwŏn Kŭn originally prepared
this diagram for two students who were
having trouble understanding Zhou
Dunyi's theory of the cosmos and Zhu Xi's
theory of the human psyche. It proved so
helpful that Kwŏn Kŭn collected it and a
number of other diagrams, with explanations, in his* Diagrams and Explanations
for Beginning Study.

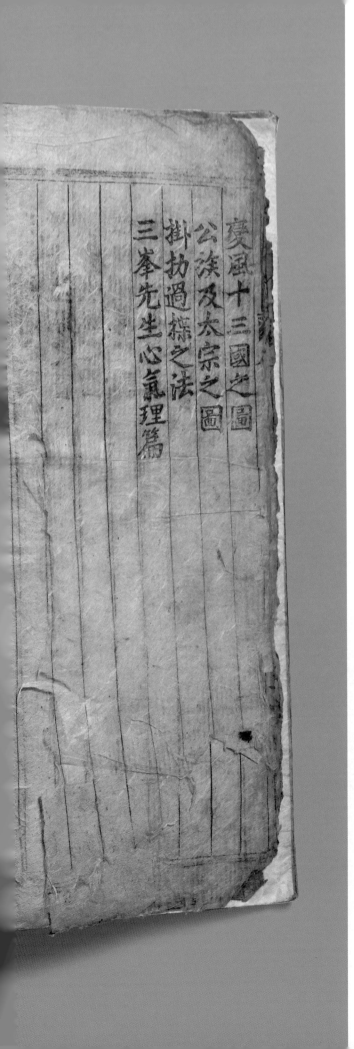

KOREAN CONFUCIANISM

From the time of its introduction into Korea, Buddhism enjoyed the favor of the ruling elite, rising to the status of state religion with the unification of the territory of Korea under Koryŏ. At the peak of Buddhist influence, in the eleventh century, one reigning king abolished the death penalty in deference to Buddhist doctrine, decreed that one son in every family with three or four or more take the tonsure, and had metal that was to have been forged into weapons cast into nails for the construction of monasteries. Five centuries later, King Chungjong would order a monumental Buddha broken up for scrap metal, temples would be closed, and Neo-Confucianism would have displaced Buddhism as the state ideology.

The transition from Koryŏ Buddhism to Chosŏn Neo-Confucianism was neither quick nor clean. Confucians had long been a presence at court, occasionally even a significant presence. But more than the growing acceptance of Confucian thought, it was a growing dissatisfaction with the institution of Buddhism—the threat of its enormous wealth and power and concomitant corruption—that fuelled the ascendance of Neo-Confucianism. A desire to align itself more closely with Ming China, a Confucian state, than with its fallen predecessor, the Yuan dynasty, whose Mongol rulers favored Buddhism, may also have contributed to Chosŏn's preference for Neo-Confucian thought.

Traditional Confucianism emphasized relationships between people: lord and minister, father and son, older and younger brother, husband and wife, friend and friend. In contrast to this outward view of morality, Neo-Confucianism looked inward, espousing cultivation of the inner self and providing a metaphysical aspect to the ethical structure of traditional Confucianism. One of the first texts to introduce the tenets of Neo-Confucianism to the Korean intelligentsia was Kwŏn Kŭn's *Iphak tosŏl, Diagrams and Explanations for Beginning Study.*

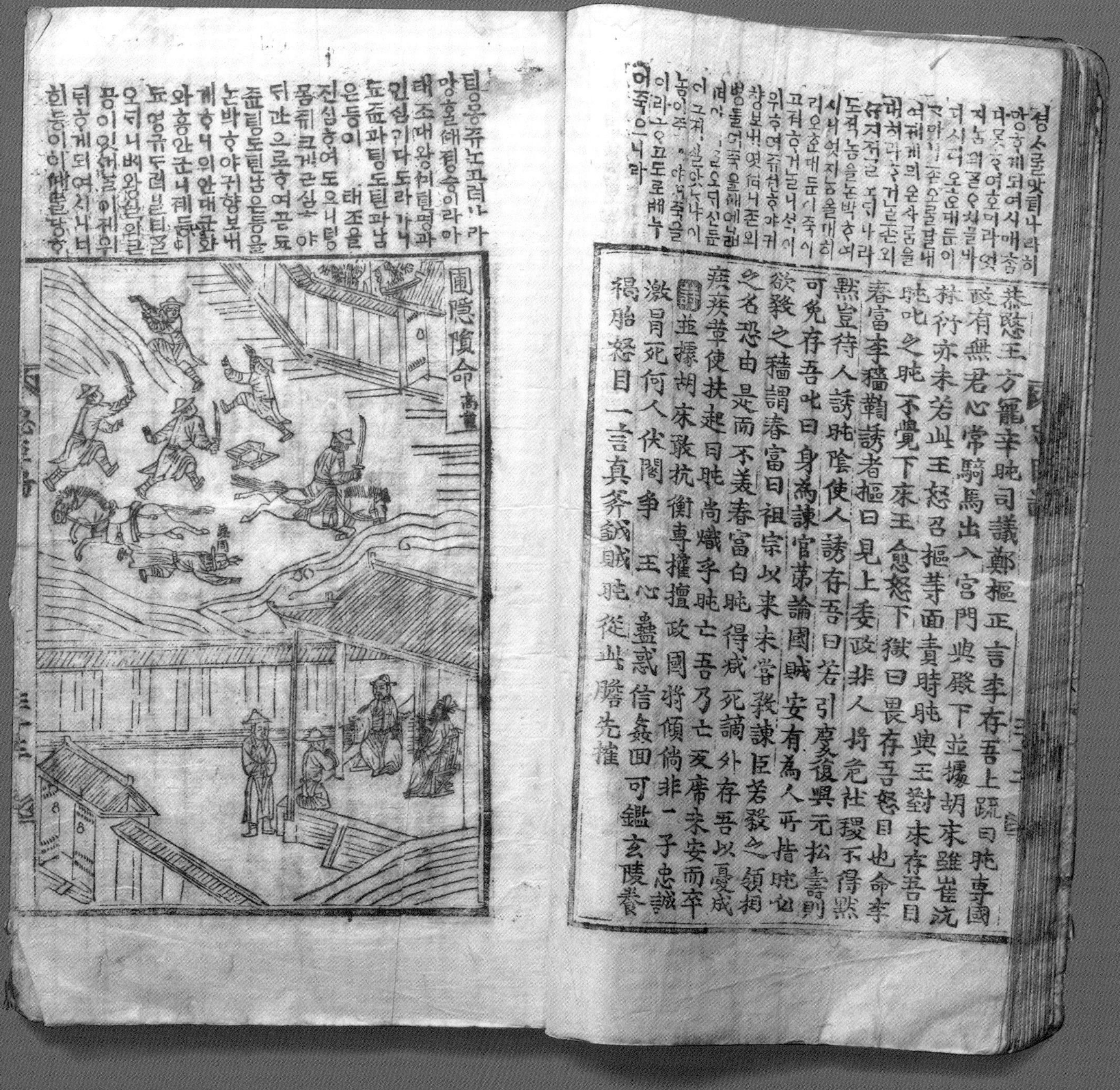

SAMGANG HAENGSILTO, COMPILED BY KYE SUN. WOODBLOCK. 1726.

The appeal of traditional Confucianism was broader than that of Neo-Confucianism, even if it was intellectually and spiritually less satisfying. This illustration is taken from a collection of biographies of exemplars of traditional Confucian virtues. Unlike most of the biographies in the collection, which relate the stories of Chinese exemplars, the tale illustrated here originated in Koryŏ.

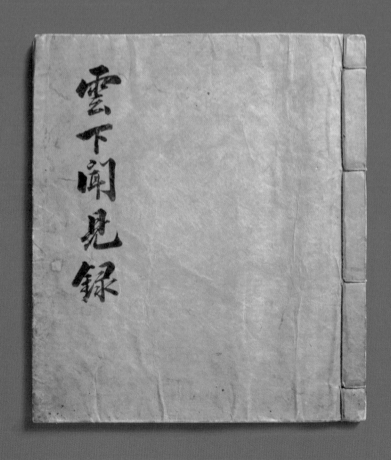

UNHA KYŎNMUNNOK, BY KIM KYU-RAK. MANUSCRIPT, IN KIM'S HAND.
CA. 1871.

One attraction of Neo-Confucianism was its potential for directing the loyalties of its adherents toward service to the state. This advantage disappeared as different strains of Korean Neo-Confucianism developed and then contended against one another. At three points during the 1860s and 1870s, the number of private Confucian academies was reduced in an attempt to impose a stricter orthodoxy and eliminate factionalism. In his manuscript account of court business, Kim Kyu-rak, who served as secretary to the father of King Kojong, writes that before the suppression, there were seventeen hundred such academies; after, a mere forty-seven.

XIANFO QIZONG, BY HONG YINGMING.
WOODBLOCK. MING DYNASTY.

Scholars tell us that the author of The
Way of Laozi *lived sometime around the
third century bc. Traditional religious
Daoism maintained that he was born
centuries earlier and reincarnated
repeatedly prior to and into the Han
dynasty. Here, the deified Laozi mounted
on the blue buffalo that carried him to the
far western borders of China, where he is
said to have converted the barbarians.*

RELIGIOUS DAOISM

The eighteenth-century Confucian editors of the great Qing treasury of Chinese literature, *Siku quanshu*, wrote somewhat harshly of Hong Yingming's *Xianfo qizong, Miracles of the Immortals and Buddhas*, in their critical notes to the collectanea. Among other things, they found the mix of two discrete traditions, Daoism and Buddhism, unacceptable. They also found much in the content that was "fantastic." They accordingly placed the work not in the Daoist section of the treasury but in the section devoted to *xiaoshuo*, "minor traditions" and fiction.

The literature of religious Daoism dates from the second century AD, when Zhang Daoling received the divine revelations that would ultimately lead to the establishment of the Celestial Masters sect. This late date didn't prevent the popular religion from claiming for its pantheon earlier quasi-historical or mythological figures such as Laozi or Xiwangmu, the tailed and saber-toothed guardian of the elixir of immortality. As religious Daoism developed, it deified later historical figures, such as the general Guan Yu, whose biography appears in the official history of the Three Kingdoms era. Eclectic in nature, popular Daoism also occasionally appropriated divinities from other religions, such as the Buddhist bodhisattva Guanyin.

As might be expected, the distinction between Daoist hagiography and fiction is frequently ambiguous, an ambiguity compounded by the general tendency of hagiography to illustrate religious or spiritual paradigms at the expense of fully rounded biography, and the particular tendency in the Daoist case to enhance certain aspects of the tales in an effort to lend them authority. Early collections of tales of the sublime were mined for whatever they contained pertaining to Daoist transcendents, and some of these collections found their way into the Daoist canon. That *Xianfo qizong* did not, might be ascribed to its late date of publication or to a lack of original source material. It could not be ascribed to a Daoist aversion to syncretism or exclusive embrace of historical fact.

"ZHANG TIANSHI XIANG BING ZAN," TEXT ATTRIBUTED TO TANG SUZONG. RUBBING. UNDATED.

One strain of religious Daoism that focused on the practice of alchemy appealed especially to the elite of medieval China. During the reign of Tang Xuanzong, it came close to being declared the state religion. The panegyric accompanying this portrait of Zhang Daoling is attributed to Xuanzong's successor, Suzong.

ACTS OF DEVOTION

Just like the recitation of a prayer, the paper-and-ink reproduction of a sutra could be an act of devotion in traditional East Asia. The act could be private, as when an individual devotee undertook the copying of a sutra by hand. It could also be public, as when a temple, possibly with the backing of a wealthy patron, issued a large printing of a sutra for mass distribution. The act could be a form of meditation, whose merit lay in the process rather than the product. It could be a votive act, performed in supplication for a particular intention or in repayment for divine assistance.

Although the reproduction yielded new copies of the sutras, it did not always serve the practical purpose of increasing the number of copies in circulation. In eleventh- and twelfth-century Japan, devotees buried sutras in mounds to preserve them against *mappō*, a future time when the world would suffer cataclysm and the Dharma would decline. In tenth-century China, the ruler of the state of Wu-Yue enclosed miniature sutras in the hollow bricks used to build the Thunder Peak Pagoda, Leifeng ta, in Hangzhou.

These texts generally include some indication of who copied the sutra or sponsored its printing, when, and why. In the case of Chinese sutras whose printing was sponsored by a number of devotees, the amount of the donation in cash, or even in kind, might be noted. The donations could be as modest as a block of wood—a sharp contrast to the obvious expense of some of the sutras produced by the medieval Japanese nobility, which incorporated precious and semiprecious materials and illustrations by professional artists.

NANZENBUSHŪ BANKOKU SHŌKA NO ZU, BY HŌTAN. WOODBLOCK. 1710.

First published in 1710, this map is descended from a line of Japanese manuscript maps based on the journey of the Chinese priest Xuanzang's pilgrimage to India in search of scriptures. Scholars believe that the maps were originally copied out as a form of devotion—a pilgrimage of the spirit if not of the body—and that later versions like this, which includes South America, demonstrate an attempt to reconcile sacred geography with the examples of European cartography that were reaching Japan through Dutch traders and, via China, Jesuit missionaries.

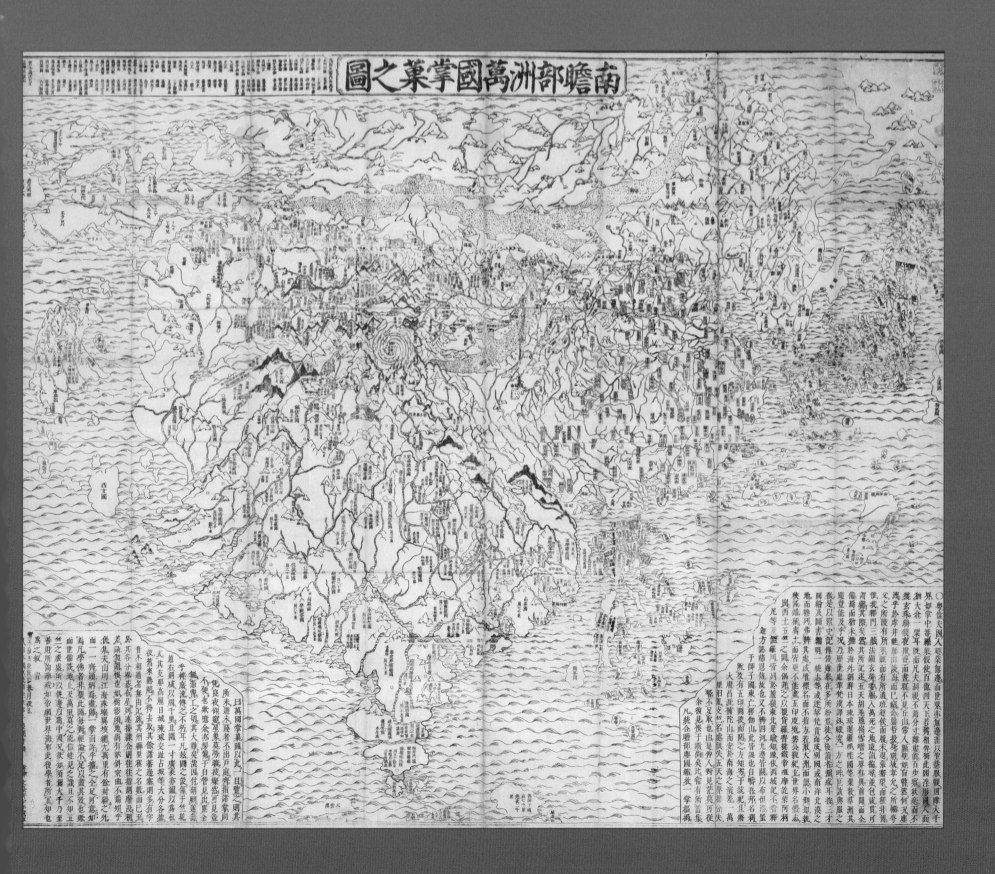

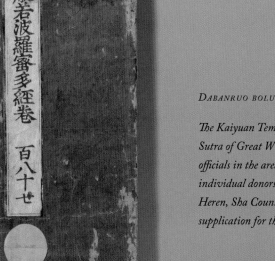

Dabanruo boluomiduo jing. Woodblock. 1115, 1345–68.

The Kaiyuan Temple of Fuzhou originally carved the blocks for this edition of the Sutra of Great Wisdom in 1115. Between 1345 and 1346, civil and military officials in the area raised funds for a new printing, which was supplemented by individual donors. The interlinear text pictured here tells us that Zeng Tieniu of Heren, Sha County, donated two blocks toward the printing of the sutra "in supplication for the preservation of peace."

MYŌHŌRENGEKYŌ. MANUSCRIPT.
UNDATED.

*This Japanese manuscript copy of the
Lotus Sutra has no elaborate frontispiece,
but the copyist's effort is apparent in the
size of the text: each character measures no
more than one millimeter in height.*

RELIGION OF IMAGES

Some faiths and sects, including early Indian Buddhism, frown on the representation of the sacred as sacrilege, profanity, or distraction. The Buddhism of traditional East Asia harbored no such inhibition. It made use of religious images and imagery to instruct and inspire its devotees, to attract converts, and even to frighten the wayward.

In China, illustration was so commonly exploited by Buddhist proselytizers that the faith became known as the "religion of images." Monks who recounted miracle stories before crowds often added appeal to their spiritual lessons by lecturing against a backdrop depicting episodes from the tale; fully illustrated editions of the most popular sutras enabled the illiterate to read; elaborate frontispieces epitomized the scriptures they preceded. But illustration need not have been accompanied by narrative text to be effective. Appended to prayers or instructional texts or to no text at all, portraits of the Buddha could serve as devotional aids, amulets could protect the carrier, depictions of hell could teach the perniciousness of karma. Representing a virtually unchanging pantheon, these images could cross political and temporal boundaries without losing their efficacy.

[OPPOSITE PAGE]

SŎKKA YŎRAE HAENGJŎK SONG.
WOODBLOCK. 1795–97.

This fifteenth-century Korean reprint of a Chinese work dating to the Yuan dynasty depicts, among others, the hell of boiling cauldrons, whose king bears a striking resemblance to a Chinese Confucian magistrate. The text above advises that this hell can be avoided by repeated invocation of the name of the Buddha of Medicine.

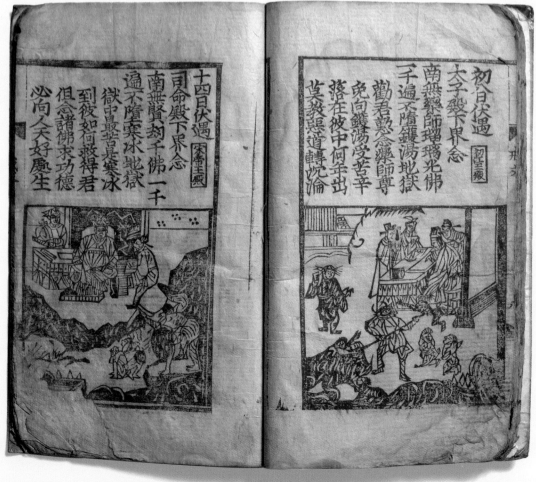

CH'ŎNJI P'ARYANG SINJU KYŎNG, TEXT ATTRIBUTED TO WUXUE.
WOODBLOCK. 15TH CENTURY.

*Śākyamuni is frequently portrayed flanked by Mañjuśrī mounted on a white
lion and Samatabhadra on an elephant, and surrounded by an audience of
lesser celestial beings. Above right, Samatabhadra, from an engraving in a
Korean edition of a collection of Chinese Buddhist tracts and incantations.*

"DAMO MIAN BI TU BING ZAN,"
TEXT, CALLIGRAPHY, AND DRAWING
BY FENGDIAN. RUBBING. UNDATED.

Rubbing of an engraving of Bodhidharma,
the first patriarch of Chinese Chan,
or Zen, Buddhism. Arriving from India
in the early decades of the seventh century,
Bodhidharma spent his first nine years in
China in contemplation seated facing a
wall. This portrait is the work of a Ming
dynasty monk, Fengdian.

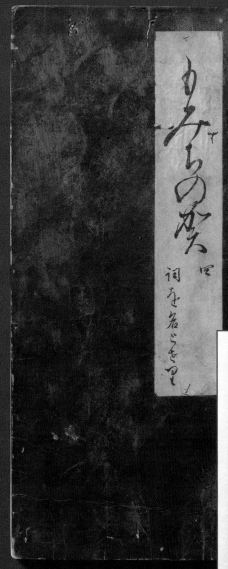

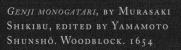

GENJI MONOGATARI, BY MURASAKI
SHIKIBU, EDITED BY YAMAMOTO
SHUNSHŌ. WOODBLOCK. 1654

Among Genji's less serious liaisons was the
aging flirt Naishi. When she coquettishly
raised her fan before her face, Genji
noticed that the color did not complement
her complexion; the inscription, moreover,
made an unfortunate allusion to age and
the loss of allure. Genji traded fans with
Naishi to spare her from again appearing
to such disadvantage.

Court, Town, and Country

The Heian court

Court documents reflect policy, and official histories, the complexities of court politics, but for a depiction of court life in Heian Japan, the authoritative source is a work of fiction, Murasaki Shikibu's *Tale of Genji*. A member by birth and marriage of the powerful Fujiwara clan, Murasaki served as lady-in-waiting to the imperial consort Shōshi just after the turn of the eleventh century. Her familiarity with court life is apparent in the pages of *Genji*, named for the fictional prince whose story it tells.

While scholars have identified the historical counterparts of the some of the novel's other characters, the attraction of Genji is not that of a roman à clef. It is rather as an intimate portrait of Genji's entanglements and emotions and how they come to bear on Genji as he ages that most readers have turned to the tale for centuries.

For the cultural historian, *Genji* holds another attraction. George Sansom, the premier historian of Japan in the West, has described the Heian as an era "governed by a rule of taste." *Genji* abounds with examples of the implementation of this rule—in the appreciation of nature, verse, calligraphy; in personal adornment and address; in the practice of piety and the rituals of romance. The Heian predilection for the austere and exquisite is also present, albeit in varying degrees, in most illustrations of the tale, whether painted screen, handscroll, or simple woodblock.

Jujō Genji, by Nonoguchi Ryūho.
Woodblock. Undated.

Genji's wife and his discarded lovers felt that dignity required them to endure his indiscretions quietly, but their attendants felt no such restraint. Meeting at the Kamo festival, they taunt one another while Genji's own men pretend to be unaware of the scuffle.

GENJI KOKAGAMI, BY FUJIWARA NAGACHIKA.
WOODBLOCK. UNDATED.

*As rarified as the atmosphere of the Heian court was,
the popularity of the* Tale of Genji *only grew with
the passage of time, although readers increasingly found
the language and the length of the novel intimidating.
Fujiwara Nagachika was the first to attempt a simplified
version of the novel with his* Genji kokagami. *First
presented to the Ashikaga shogun Yoshimochi around 1423,
the digested version of* Genji *went through numerous
editions and printings in the sixteenth century.*

KŬMO KYECH'ŎP. INK AND COLOR
ON SILK. 1745–1805.

*The primary function of court painters
under the Chosŏn dynasty was to produce
commemorative albums of court ceremonies
and festivities. Under the authority of
the Ministry of Rites, court painters
worked collectively and in a style that was
prescriptively archaic. Pictured here is a
painting commemorating the initiation
of new judges into the Ŭigŭmbu, or High
Court. The building was sacrificed to
modernization in the first decade of the
twentieth century.*

CHOSŎN SEOUL

Legend has it that the old city walls of Seoul were laid out along a line of
snowdrifts created by a stiff wind one night shortly after the city had been
established as the capital of the Chosŏn dynasty. Similarly dictated by
nature were the siting and design of one of the three eastern gates in those
walls, the Ogan Sumun, whose five arches spanned the Ch'ŏnggyech'ŏn,
a channel fed by mountain creeks and flowing into the Han River. The
stream drained runoff during Seoul's rainy season and carried away sewage
year-round, alternating between flooding and fetidness. Sedimentation
aggravated the problem as the years passed and the city grew.

In 1760, two hundred thousand men worked for over two months to
dredge the stream. Completion of the project was marked with official
banquets and an archery contest on the palace grounds. The dredging
so improved conditions for the inhabitants of the capital that King Yŏngjo
appointed a commission to oversee regular dredging and had the banks
of the stream reinforced with stone.

In spite of this, by the early decades of the twentieth century the stream
had once again become a health hazard, and by the sixties the space
occupied by the stream's bed and banks was needed to ease the flow
of traffic in the modern city. Concrete slabs were laid over the
Ch'ŏnggyech'ŏn and an elevated highway built above it. More recently,
the slabs have been removed, the waterway rehabilitated, and a bit of
Seoul's past restored to the present.

CHUNCH'ŎN KYECH'ŎP. INK AND COLOR ON SILK. CA. 1760?

This painting occurs in an album made to commemorate the dredging and the official celebrations that followed its completion. Here, King Yŏngjo and his entourage watch the work from the top of the Ogan Sumun, in the vicinity of the present Dongdaemun market.

Kyō warabe, by Nakagawa Kiun. Woodblock. 1658.

The Seiryō-ji stood out among the temples of the Kyoto area for its fine image of Śākyamuni. This illustration strays from the text in suggesting that the temple's main attraction was its guardian figures. It further strays in depicting the aggressive behavior of teahouse hostesses, even if the characterization is accurate. Kyō warabe *is frequently cited as one of the earliest examples of the* meisho ki *genre.*

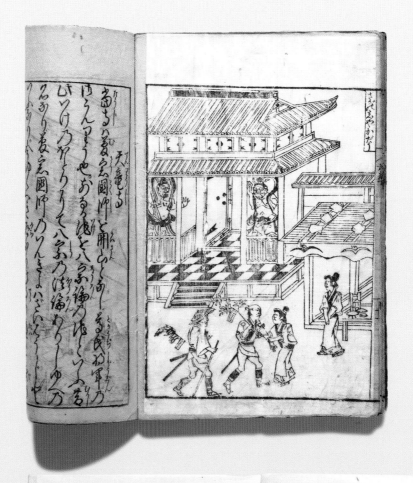

Shui Miyako meisho zue, by Akizato Ritō, illustrated by Takehara Shunchōsai. Woodblock. 1787.

The muskmelons of the village of Toba, now in the Minami ward of Kyoto, were one of the celebrated products of the region. The extravagance of the illustration, the sparseness of the text, the bulk of the work in which the woodblock appears (six volumes) would never be found in a travel guide intended for practical use.

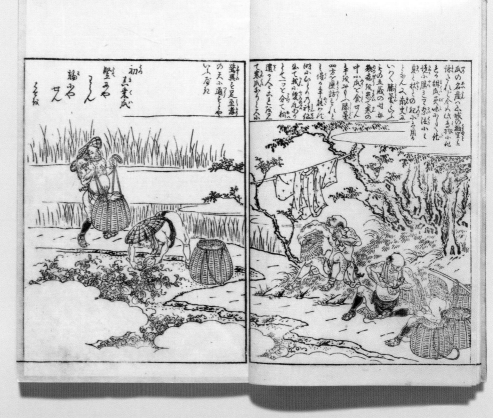

CELEBRATED PLACES

Insular and deliberately seclusionist, Tokugawa Japan did not begin to produce the volumes on foreign exploration that Europe did in the seventeenth and eighteenth centuries. Instead, Kyoto publishers chose to evoke the small pleasures of the everyday world around them in a genre known as *meisho ki*, "records of celebrated places," and later in *meisho zue*, "illustrations" of the same. In origin, the works were intended as tourists' or pilgrims' guides dedicated to particular shrines, routes, or cities and providing information on their respective attractions. The resulting emphasis was on the local and the current. Over time—in response, some believe, to the success Edo publishers had selling light fiction and guides to the pleasure quarters illustrated by *ukiyo-e* artists—the books came to contain as much pictorial as textual content, and to court the interests of the armchair traveler as much as the tourist.

Characteristic of *meisho zue* illustration are bird's-eye views of towns and temple complexes, but the artists regularly descended to street level. With their detail, humor, and air of the everyday, Hasegawa Settan's frequently reproduced woodblocks of Edo's busiest bridge, Nihonbashi, or the nearby fish market appear to have more in common with genre painting than with landscape. Similarly, Shunchōsai's illustrations of the capital in *Miyako meisho zue* reflect the seasonal cycle of life in the city and surrounding countryside. Modern scholars have complained that by neglecting what is not picturesque, the *meisho zue* offer an incomplete picture of contemporary life. They nonetheless hold a wealth of information for the social historian, as at least one *meisho zue* author, Akizato Ritō, intended they would. "If we don't set down a clear record of today, today," he wrote, "later generations will become ever more ignorant of whatever remains of it. How regrettable that would be!"

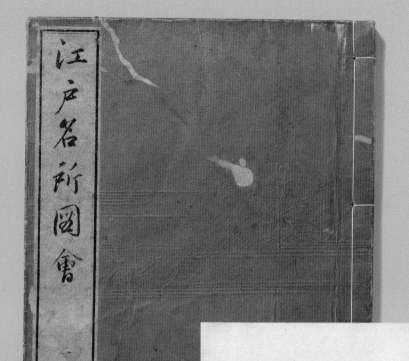

Tōto meisho zue, by Saitō Chōshū, illustrated by
Hasegawa Settan. Woodblock. 1834–36

*Shops selling metalware and equestrian trappings in the vicinity of the
main gate to the Yoshiwara ward. The shop sign on the far right, displaying door pulls and decorative hardware, identifies the establishment while
advertising the quality of the goods sold. In front of the shops, a vendor
hawks rice dumplings, and passersby watch draymen strain to haul a
temple bell through the sloping street.*

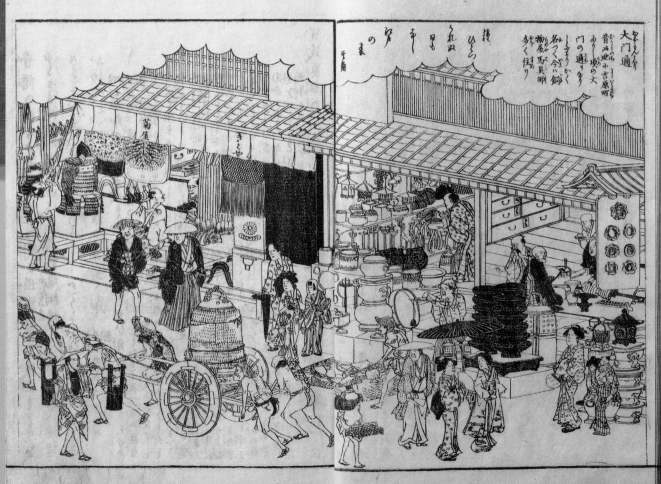

Narita meisho zue, by Nakaji Sadatoshi and Nakaji Sadanori, illustrated by Hasegawa Settei. Woodblock. 1858.

While foreigners were forbidden to acquire maps and other works on Japan's geography and government for fear they would reveal too much about Japan's vulnerabilities, eighteen meisho zue *were sent for display at the Paris Exposition Universelle of 1867, and two were presented to Napoleon III earlier in the decade. Here, from one of the works presented, is the annual roundup of wild horses at Shimono.*

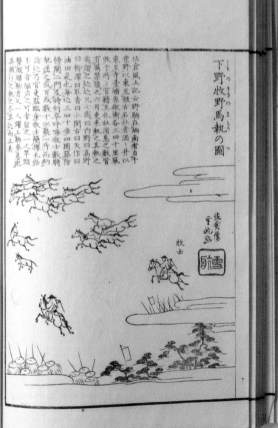

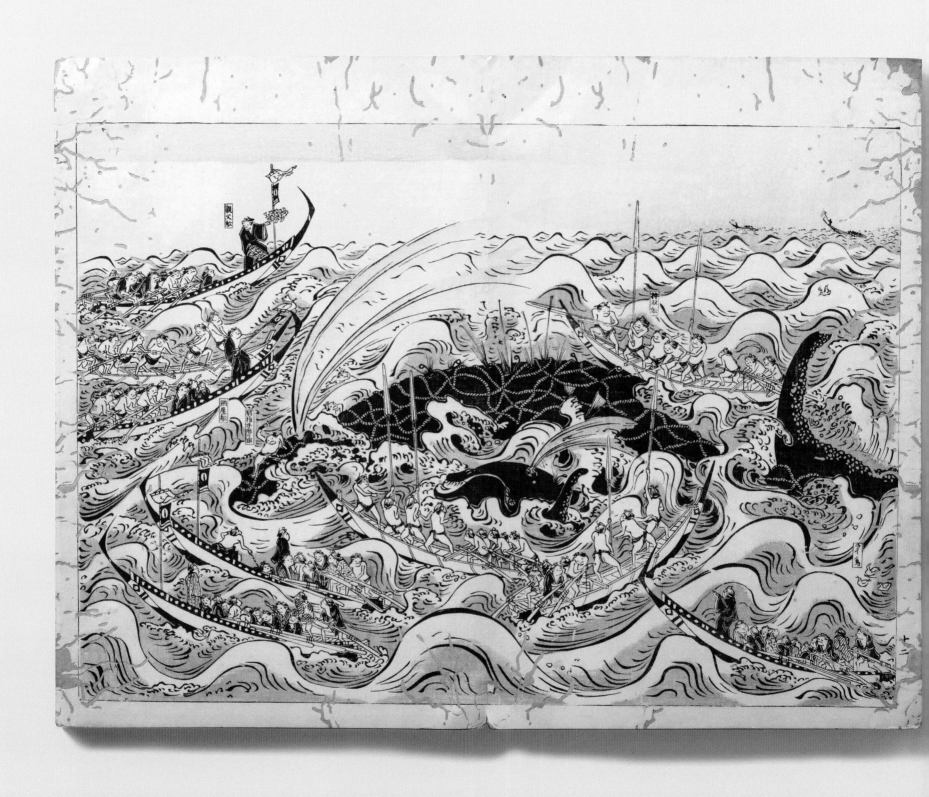

Whales and whaling

Whaling was a profitable enterprise for some in premodern Europe and America but not always an economical one. At times the mammal was hunted for nothing more than its blubber and bone. The naturalist Engelbert Kaempfer, an early visitor to Japan, was therefore surprised to see just how efficiently the Japanese mined the resource. "Nothing of these whales is thrown away as useless," he wrote. The preface from the earliest Japanese monograph on whales, *Geishi*, is more specific: "That all its parts, from its skin, flesh, sinews, and bones, to its guts and offal, are of vast use and benefit to the common people, is commonly known."

Another distinguishing feature of traditional Japanese whaling is that it was shore-based. On the small island of Ikitsuki, to cite a specific case, lookouts manned watch stations along the coast and on islets from which whales could be spotted. On sighting one, the watch raised a signal flag, sending small, swift boats to the water, where they encircled the whale and chased it into a net stretched between boats. Once the whale was netted and secured, harpooners moved in. The kill was then towed to shore, where flensers and others began their work, carrying away nets or stripping off lengths of blubber, perhaps with the aid of windlasses. Processing continued in nearby sheds. Preparations occupied the pre-season, when rope was twisted, boats mended, harpoons sharpened or newly forged.

Until the mid-nineteenth century and the intrusion of whalers from America and Europe, whales, especially right whales, were plentiful in the waters west of Japan. The gift was not taken for granted. Japanese anciently called the whale *gyoō*, the "king of sea creatures," referring not only to its size but its usefulness. Men of science, like the author of *Geishi*, distinguished whale species and their respective characteristics. Communities that relied on whaling erected funerary tablets and shrines to commemorate whales killed for subsistence. One Buddhist temple, Kōgan-ji, in Kayoi, even maintained rolls of the dead and to this day holds annual memorial services for the souls of whales taken in the hunt.

Isanatori ekotoba, by Oyamada Tomokiyo. Woodblock. 1829.

The net was introduced around the end of the seventeenth century. Before that, Japanese whalers simply harpooned their prey from boats. Before that, inhabitants of coastal areas harvested whales only when they happened to wash onto shore. Here, an Ikitsuki harpooner cuts a hole through which rope will be drawn to secure the whale.

GEISHI, BY YAMASE HARUYASA. WOODBLOCK. 1760.

The right whale, from Yamase Haruyasa's Geishi. *Although highly praised and reprinted, Yamase's work was faulted by some, including one reader of this copy. It nevertheless remained an authoritative source for many years. Philipp von Siebold, who visited Japan in the nineteenth century, sent a copy of* Geishi *and a manuscript Dutch translation of the treatise back to Europe, where he used it in writing his own account of Japan's fauna.*

TŌKAIDŌ NARABINI SAIGOKU DŌCHŪ EMAKI. HANDSCROLL, INK AND COLOR
ON PAPER. 1700.

*As coastal waters became depleted, many traditional whaling stations gave up
the hunt or traveled to distant waters in search of whales. Whalers from the Gotō
Archipelago, just southwest of Ikitsuki in Nagasaki Prefecture, have hunted as far
away as the Antarctic.*

經

素絲頭緒多羨君
好安排青黳不動
塵緩步交去來脈
脈意欲亂卷々首
重回王言正如絲
亦付經綸才

TILLING AND WEAVING

Agriculture and industry form the foundation of almost any developed economy. In premodern China, this foundation was epitomized in the phrase *gengzhi,* "tilling and weaving." What was most widely cultivated, of course, was rice; and what was most profitably woven was silk.

The Song dynasty literatus Lou Shou developed an intense interest in rice cultivation and sericulture while serving as county magistrate in the region west of modern-day Hangzhou. Observing the seasonal cycle of each, he also came to appreciate the physical hardships each entailed. In 1145 Lou Shou presented his observations to the imperial throne in a series of paintings with accompanying verse. The compilation was later engraved in stone. A prefect in the area southeast of modern Hangzhou, one Wang Gang, also had it engraved onto woodblocks for printing and distribution. His aim was to instill in the more privileged strata of society an appreciation of the efforts expended to fill their bellies and clothe them.

In 1696, the Kangxi emperor, inspired by Lou Shou's work, ordered the Qing court painter Jiao Bingzhen to execute a series of paintings devoted to the same subject. The emperor himself contributed verse, and Zhu Gui, an engraver of high reputation, translated the whole into woodblock.

Jiao based his paintings roughly on Lou Shou's. Most editions of the imperially sponsored *Gengzhi tu, Pictures of Tilling and Weaving,* preserve Lou Shou's verse as well. In his preface to the work, the Kangxi emperor acknowledged sympathies akin to Lou Shou's. The deliberate correspondence between the two works implies that the emperor was as familiar with his realm as the Song magistrate was with his county, and as concerned with moral instruction as the later prefect, Wang Gang.

Scholars have suggested that the emperor might have had a broader political purpose in producing *Gengzhi tu.* The Qing dynasty was established by Manchu tribesmen eager not simply to conquer China but to become Chinese. By the Kangxi era, the Han population had resigned itself to foreign rule, and the Manchu elite had assimilated its subjects' language, culture, and values. The illustrations of *nan geng, nü zhi,* "men tilling and women weaving," of productive labor and social order, might have been meant as attestation to both the success of the Kangxi reign and the thoroughness of the Manchu sinification. At the same time, the Manchu sovereign was aligning himself with centuries of Chinese emperors, who with their consorts had annually presided over rites honoring the gods of agriculture and sericulture, thereby assuring continued peace and prosperity in the empire.

PEIWEN GENGZHI TU, BY LOU SHOU, QING SHENGZU, AND QING SHIZONG, ILLUSTRATED BY JIAO BINGZHEN. 1892.

Art historians like to note that in his tilling and weaving paintings Jiao Bingzhen employed Western perspective, absorbed from the European Jesuits he associated with at the Qing court. The painter also had an eye for detail. Here, twisting warp threads on a multiple-spindle doubling-frame.

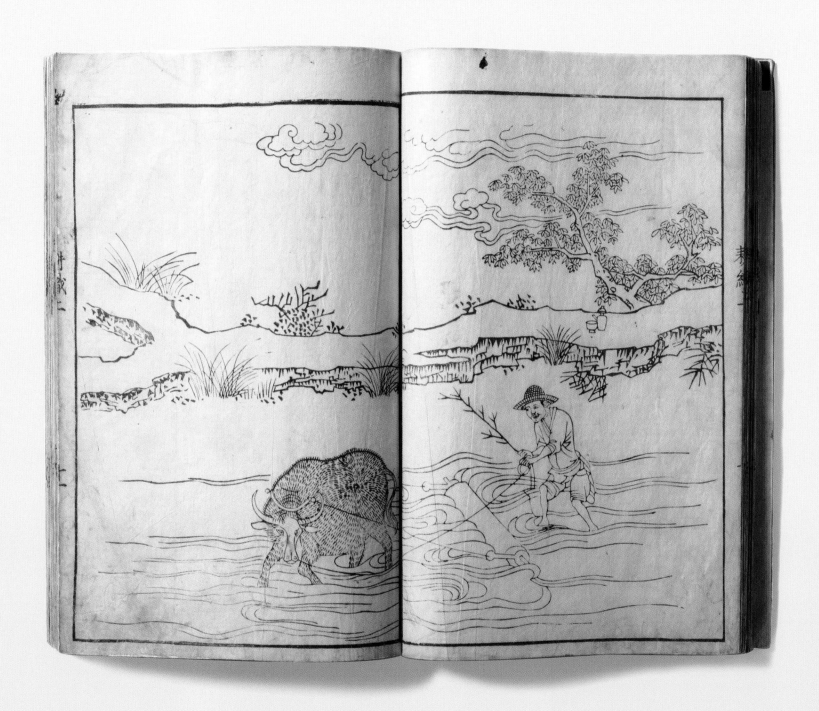

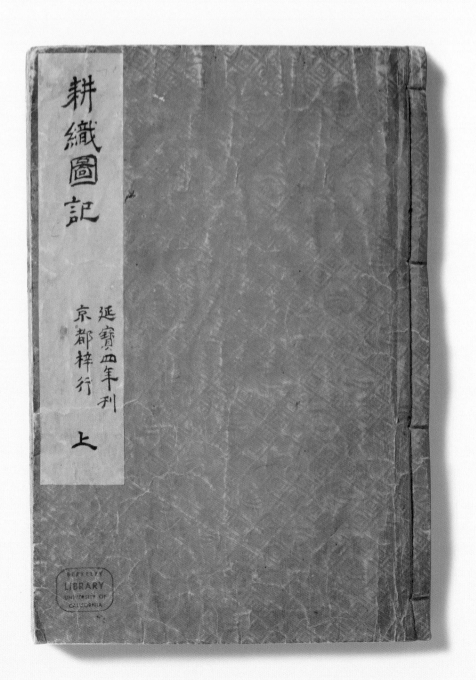

Koshoku zuki, TEXT AND ILLUSTRATIONS
BY LOU SHOU. WOODBLOCK. 1676.

*Although extant into the eighteenth century, by the
early twentieth Lou Shou's pictures and poems of
tilling and weaving could not be found in China.
Fortunately, they had survived in Japan, in a
seventeenth-century republication of the 1462
edition of Lou Shou's work, an edition scholars agree
is faithful to Wang Gang's thirteenth-century edition.
To the left, leveling the ground with an ox-drawn roller.*

THE PURSUIT OF PLEASURE

EHON

"The pleasantest of all diversions is to sit alone under the lamp, a book spread out before you, and to make friends with people of a distant past you have never known," the priest Kenkō writes in *Tsurezuregusa, Essays in Idleness*. The work, which includes close to two hundred and fifty short sketches and reflections, is of the genre called *zuihitsu*, seemingly random writings that "follow the brush." The writings are "seemingly" random, since some critics see method and thematic unity in such collections where others see none. Yet both camps would have to agree that the name of the genre indicates a degree of self-indulgence in the act of writing. Kenkō points to this in the opening passage of his *Essays*—"I have spent whole days before this inkstone, with nothing better to do, jotting down at random whatever nonsensical thoughts have entered my head"—suggesting that there was pleasure in the indulgence as well.

Kenkō wrote his *Essays* in the early 1330s, and they have been enjoyed since by readers of all sorts, young and old, well and less educated. The miscellany's popularity has been explained by its inclusiveness, its exclusiveness, its didacticism, its sensual appeal, its philosophical and spiritual overtones, its refusal to wax too profound. What is apparent, even to the uninitiated, is the ability of Kenkō's prose to elicit a variety of responses from a variety of readers. It was perhaps that evocative power of Kenkō's language, along with the familiarity of the work, that led the *ukiyo-e* artist Nishikawa Sukenobu to prepare an *ehon* version of the work.

[PAGE 118 AND ABOVE]

EHON TSUREZUREGUSA, BY KENKŌ, ILLUSTRATED BY NISHIKAWA SUKENOBU. 1740.

"A flute made from a sandal a woman has worn will infallibly summon the autumn deer." Kenkō's subject is the potency of passion; Sukenobu's is the female form. Sukenobu was especially known for his paintings and illustrations of bijin, *"beautiful women." The conclusion of Kenkō's essay, not reprinted in the* ehon, *warns against allowing oneself to be deluded by the senses.*

Ehon, or "picture books," developed after the emergence of commercial printing in Japan to satisfy the urban demand for books that could be enjoyed without a great deal of education on the part of the buyer. Pictures dominate the page, text is minimal or absent. The printer's colophon in this edition of *Ehon Tsurezuregusa* demonstrates this dominance: it names Sukenobu as the artist, Yamamoto Kihei as the engraver (an unusual credit), and Kikuya Kihei as the publisher of the work; it does not name the author Kenkō. The *ehon* includes only a selection of Kenkō's sketches and meditations, and generally only the opening passages of the meditations selected.

It is true that the author of *Tsurezuregusa* did not need to be named—in his preface to the *ehon*, Sukenobu refers to Kenkō simply as "the Buddhist priest." It is equally true that for readers familiar with Kenkō's *Essays*, the opening passages reprinted in the *ehon* provide mnemonic enough to recall the whole. They apparently supplied inspiration enough to Sukenobu, whose woodcut illustrations created a book even the illiterate could take pleasure in.

Closet drama

Chinese drama, an operatic entertainment, was performed publicly during the Yuan dynasty. The dramatic texts printed at that time are believed to have been chiefly play scripts and libretti produced for the use of actors and audience. By the Ming dynasty, however, drama was being read privately, and avidly, in editions designed for readers of all tastes.

Publishers responding to this readership marketed books of varying quality and format. Some were illustrated with part-, full-, or double-page wood-cuts. Some were printed with "eyebrow commentary" in the upper margin above the text, where readers often added their own remarks in brush and ink. For the aficionado, there were recensions whose text had been edited to ensure that, as Zang Maoxun put it, "action and mood were properly paired and rhyme was consonant with melody." For serious or insatiable readers, there were appendices of special interest: critiques, the texts of literary precursors to the drama, skits habitually performed with the featured drama. Some of these recensions were edited by men of significant literary or intellectual authority, such as Zang Maoxun or Li Zhi (better known to the book-buying public as Li Zhuowu).

There were derivative works as well. The Qing dynasty *Yaqu cangshu*, for instance, reproduced illustrations from a published edition of *Xixiang ji*, *Tale of the Western Wing*, but in place of the drama's text presented verse and prose inspired by it. Commercial publishers also issued illustrated anthologies that collected excerpts from the works of selected playwrights.

Commentary and marginalia reveal that many of these editions retained an affiliation with performance in the minds of both their editors and readers. Nor have literary historians found any evidence that the increasing popularity of reading plays led to a decline in their performance. One has even compared the purchase and reading of dramatic texts to another Ming phenomenon, the rise in the private performance of popular drama.

本是織
女牽牛誰料做
參辰卯酉

HONGLI JI, BY XU FUZUO, FROM *SHENYIN JIANGU LU*. WOODBLOCK. PRINTED
BEFORE 1834, FROM UNDATED BLOCKS.

Tale of the Red Pear, *by the Ming playwright Xu Fuzuo, from a Qing anthology of*
drama with exceptionally fine illustrations. Here, the courtesan Xie Suqiu and the
scholar Zhao Ruzhou. The inscription, taken from one of the play's arias, compares
the beauty and the scholar to the most famous lovers of Chinese legend, Weaving Girl
and Herd Boy.

NANKE JI, BY TANG XIANZU, FROM *YUMING XINCI SIZHONG*, EDITED BY ZANG MAOXUN. WOODBLOCK. 1618.

From his editorial comments, it is clear that Zang Maoxun meant to address the interests of both reader and theatergoer in his recension of playwright Tang Xianzu's works. The illustrations in this edition of the plays, however, cater to readers who don't use the stage as their frame of reference. Here, scenes from Tale of the Southern Branch.

Li Zhuowu xiansheng piping Xixiang ji, by Wang Shifu, edited by Li Zhi. Woodblock. After 1573.

The large, bold characters enclosed in cartouches identify the tunes to which the lyrics, following, were to be sung. Dialog appears in smaller, lighter characters, while stage directions, similarly small and light, are enclosed in cartouches. One past reader of this copy of Tale of the Western Wing *clearly enjoyed the passage in which the male lead describes the symptoms of lovesickness, as well as Li Zhuowu's comment on the passage: "His entire body has gone limp."*

[OPPOSITE PAGE]

Xixiang ji, by Wang Shifu, illustrations attributed to Qiu Ying, calligraphy attributed to Wen Zhengming. Ink and color on silk. Undated.

The most popular of all Chinese dramas, the romantic comedy Tale of the Western Wing *tells the story of a promising scholar and a young girl of good family who meet, fall in love, and defy Confucian convention when her mother refuses to let them marry. Here, the girl visits the scholar in a dream.*

INK CAKES

The four essentials of the traditional scholar's studio were paper, writing brush, inkstone, and ink. The ink was solid, often in the form of a stick. The rhythmic exercise of grinding the stick on the stone with water, added drop by drop, determined the consistency of the liquid ink. It also gave the scholar time to collect his thoughts or let them roam. Because the exercise as well as the ink lent so much to the aesthetic experience of composition, writing, and reading, scholars came to set great store by the ink they used. Some even made their own ink or took an active part in making it.

The basic recipe for Chinese ink calls for mixing together blackening and a binding agent, kneading it, pressing it into a mold, and letting it dry. The results varied widely, depending on the quality of the ingredients and the specific techniques employed. The most commonly used glue, for instance, was derived from ox hide, horn, and hooves; the choicest, according to early works on ink, derived from deer antler. How, and for how long, the ingredients were blended, kneaded, and cured all affected the final product and not inconsequentially varied from ink maker to ink maker.

The finished ink was judged from a number of aspects: its color, consistency, weight, sound, smell. Connoisseurs considered its age (the older, the better). During the Ming and Qing dynasties, they might have considered its artistic value: the calligraphy and pictorial designs pressed into its surface; the color and gilt that was occasionally applied; the shape and contours of the cake, which ranged from simple oblongs and circles to fish, bamboo shoots, bells, and apricot blossoms.

The vogue for ink made to be admired and collected rather than ground and used originated with two ink makers of the Ming dynasty, Cheng Dayue and his protégé Fang Yulu. Some of their ink cakes have been preserved in collections; hundreds more have survived in effigy if not in fact in the catalogs Cheng and Fang themselves compiled. The cakes reproduced in *Master Fang's Catalog of Ink Cakes* and *Master Cheng's Catalog of Ink Cakes* are liberal in subject matter and style, are designed by well-known artists, and allude to everything from the Confucian classics to Christian miracle stories. Both catalogs are considered among the finest examples of Chinese bookmaking.

Artistic and romantic rivalry is said to have turned Cheng Dayue against Fang Yulu. Cheng's acrimony toward Fang is openly expressed in certain passages in his catalog, published twenty years after Fang's. In an obvious attempt at one-upmanship, Cheng's catalog is greater in length, includes a great number of laudatory inscriptions by the most eminent literati, and generally strives to characterize its compiler as an artist and intellectual of greater scope than Fang Yulu. Both men claimed ink making as an avocation rather than a trade; whether it gave them pleasure is more difficult to say.

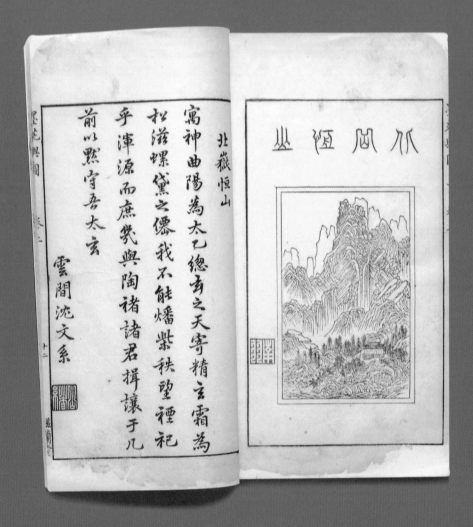

CHENG SHI MOYUAN, COMPILED BY
CHENG DAYUE, ILLUSTRATED BY
DING YUNPENG. WOODBLOCK. 1606.

*"Mount Heng, the Northern Peak," one of
the five sacred peaks of China, traditional
sites of the imperial sacrifices. The artist,
Ding Yunpeng, also known as Nanyu, is
identified by the printed seal to the left
of the ink cake. Ding designed many of
the inks in Cheng Dayue's catalog. He
was also the master of Wu Tingyu,
designer of the Fang ink cake pictured
below.*

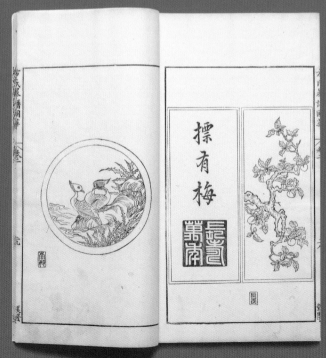

FANG SHI MOPU, COMPILED BY FANG
YULU, ILLUSTRATED BY WU TINGYU.
WOODBLOCK. 1589.

*"The plums are dropping." This page from
Fang Yulu's catalog shows both sides of the
ink cake, one pressed with a branch of
fruiting plum, the other with the verse
from the Confucian* Book of Songs *that
the plum illustrates. The artist, Wu Tingyu,
"Master Zuoqian," is identified by the
small seal reproduced in the woodblock
below the plum. The engraver's name
appears outside the frame of the page proper.*

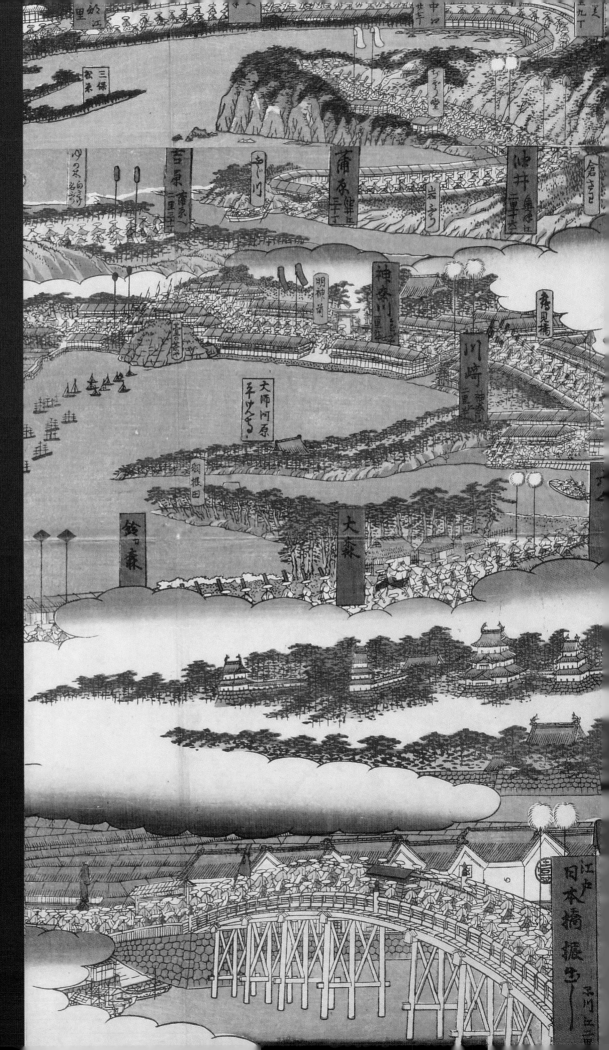

TŌKAIDŌ GYŌRETSU SUGOROKU, BY
GOUNTEI SADAHIDE, ENGRAVED BY
TANAKA TETSUYA AND TANAKA
USHINOSUKE. WOODBLOCK. 1860.

*Nihonbashi, Edo's busiest bridge, appears
in this detail from a board game–like
rendering of the Tōkaidō. The uniformed
and armed travelers filling the bridge and
the road beyond are meant to represent the
entourage of a daimyo returning to his fief
after mandatory attendance in Edo.*

THE TŌKAIDŌ

Before the 1868 Meiji Restoration and the modernization and Westernization of Japan, officials, merchants, and pilgrims traveling between Kyoto and Edo walked, rode, or were carried in palanquins along the Eastern Sea Road, the Tōkaidō.

The Tōkaidō was one in a system of five roads maintained by the Tokugawa shogunate primarily for official travel and transport. When rehabilitating the old road, the founder of the Tokugawa, Ieyasu, established military bases along the Tōkaidō and saw to it that the castles bordering its course belonged to loyal daimyo, who were charged with patrolling sections of the route. These measures worked together to ensure the state of the road and the safety of travelers. The shogunate further facilitated travel by establishing post-stations where official travelers could be assured of finding fresh horses and accommodations appropriate to their rank and standing, whether high or low.

The rise in official traffic under the Tokugawa—especially the periodical processions of daimyo whose uncertain loyalty required them to spend every other year in attendance on the shogun in Edo—stimulated the local and larger domestic economies to such a degree that commercial traffic also increased significantly on the Tōkaidō. Cheaper inns and teahouses catering to non-official travelers proliferated in the post-stations and villages. Many stations became known for products or sights unique to each: the grated yam broth of Mariko, the clams of Kuwana, the dyed textiles of Narumi and nearby Arimatsu.

Ascetic pilgrims had always been a presence on Japan's roads, but the Tokugawa improvements in travel, and perhaps the attractions of travel, drew a new type of pilgrim, the lay pilgrim, in droves. The lay pilgrim was commonly perceived to be traveling only ostensibly to visit holy sites, using the pretext of pilgrimage to circumvent restrictions on travel. The true aim of the lay pilgrims' travel was strictly pleasure, one critic wrote: "Of course, they visit the Ise Shrine, but only because it is…on the route… to Kyoto, Osaka, and Nara."

The best-known lay pilgrims to have traveled the Tōkaidō are the questionable heroes of *Shank's Mare*, a comic tale whose acknowledged purpose, unlike the secular pilgrimage's, was entertainment. Much of the novel's humor revolves around language: because the travelers are always on the move, and not always in the highest of circles, the dialog abounds with dialect, regionalisms, and slang, which are exploited for their comic potential, as is nearly every circumstance the travelers find themselves in. Published serially, the original work has gone through countless editions, printings, and avatars, and remains popular today.

The late nineteenth-century Meiji government lifted the Tokugawa restriction on travel, but it also put an end to the type of travel portrayed in *Shank's Mare*. Railway tracks were laid on much of the road; highways followed. The development that ensued engulfed some stations on the route and choked off others. Yet enough of the old Tōkaidō remains that it can be walked by those who find pleasure in seeking the past.

Ekiro no suzu. Woodblock. 1709.

A number of rivers crossed the path of the Tōkaidō. Travelers forded or were ferried from bank to bank or, when the streams were swollen, were carried across on the backs of porters familiar with the crossing. Here, the occupied palanquin, the travelers' dress, and the weapons suggest an official entourage.

TŌKAIDŌ-CHŪ HIZAKURIGE, BY JIPPENSHA IKKU, ILLUSTRATED BY
JIPPENSHA. WOODBLOCK. CA. 1865?

In a favorite scene from Shank's Mare, *here drawn in author Jippensha
Ikku's own hand, one of the novel's travelers is bitten by a turtle he had been
hoping to eat.*

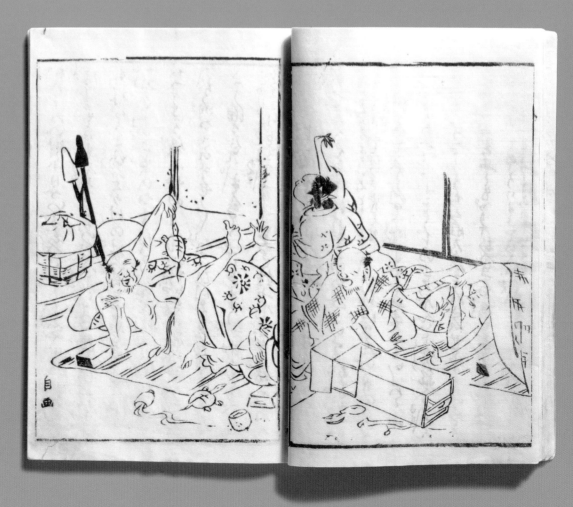

Tōkaidō narabini Saigoku dōchū ezu, by Komaki Mino.
Handscroll, ink and color on paper. 1687.

*Fuchū—birthplace of Jippensha Ikku, nineteenth of the original fifty-three
post-stations on the Tōkaidō, and the site of Tokugawa Ieyasu's Sumpu Castle.
Ieyasu spent part of his youth and ultimately the last years of his life here. Sumpu
also served as one of the shogunate's military strongholds on the Tōkaidō.*

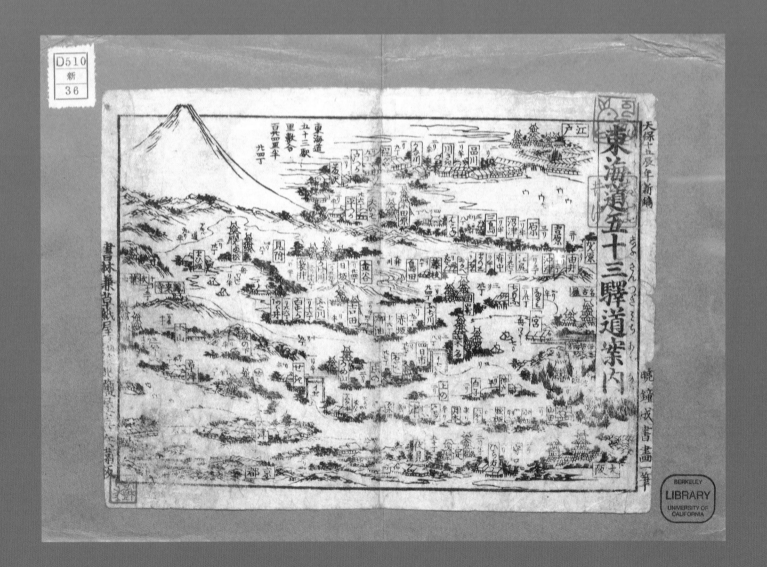

Tōkaidō gojūsantsugi michi annai, by Akatsuki Kanenari.
Woodblock. 1844.

The fifty-three stages of the Tōkaidō were roughly five and a half miles distant from one another. The road was lined with pines and paved with stone or finished with crushed granite and sand. This 1844 map, with Edo in the upper right and Kyoto in the lower left, gives equal prominence, in the lower right, to Osaka, neither beginning point, end point, or post-station—suggesting the importance the commercial center had achieved by that time, thanks in part to the trade daimyo engaged in to finance their travel on the Tōkaidō as well as their alternate residences in Edo.

Wordplay

The civil service examinations of Koryŏ and Chosŏn Korea, like those of imperial China, required that the successful candidate possess a ready and fluid ability to write, both in forms that might be used for drafting official documents and in verse. From the Confucian viewpoint, poetry was the language of diplomacy: commonly understood expressions and allusions facilitated communication, especially indirect communication.

Officially, Korean civil servants dealing with Chinese diplomatic missions had to be able to exchange poetry with their counterparts. Privately, Korean literati who espoused Neo-Confucian thought wrote verse as a form of self-cultivation. Additionally or alternatively, they borrowed Chinese poetic forms for the usual reasons poets write: to express emotions, record experiences, describe nature, comment on the world around them.

Verse and versifying could also be a source of amusement, though not always simple amusement. At court, officials exchanged verses with their ruler or one another and engaged in competitions, writing under rules that might fix the subject matter or rhyme or limit the time allowed for composition. This was more difficult than it might seem. Literary Chinese is a laconic language, capable of a good deal of syntactic and lexical flexibility; but the formal requirements of the most popular form of Chinese poetry, regulated verse, could be quite complex, reaching to imagery as well as prosody.

In less formal situations, simpler games might be played. One sort presented readers with a pattern or grid composed of characters that if read correctly would yield a series of verses comprising a poem.

It is no coincidence that some of those patterns resemble verbal patchworks. The game traces its origin to the story of Su Hui, the wife of a Chinese official posted to Central Asia during the fourth century. According to tradition, Su Hui expressed her longing for her absent husband in a series of two hundred poems, which she wove into a square of brocade the size of a handkerchief. The reader's eyes had to work their way around the cloth in various directions in order to read the poem, a device meant to mirror the turnings of the writer's heart as much as to amuse the reader.

[OPPOSITE PAGE]

HAMYŎNG [KYUBANG MIDAM]. MANUSCRIPT. UNDATED.

With this pattern, the reader starts with the smaller characters, reading from the upper right and around, in a clockwise spiral. The poem concludes with the larger characters, which are similarly read clockwise, from the outside in. The Korean manuscript in which this game appears includes a number of similar games, all sharing the common theme of the lonely wife's plaint.

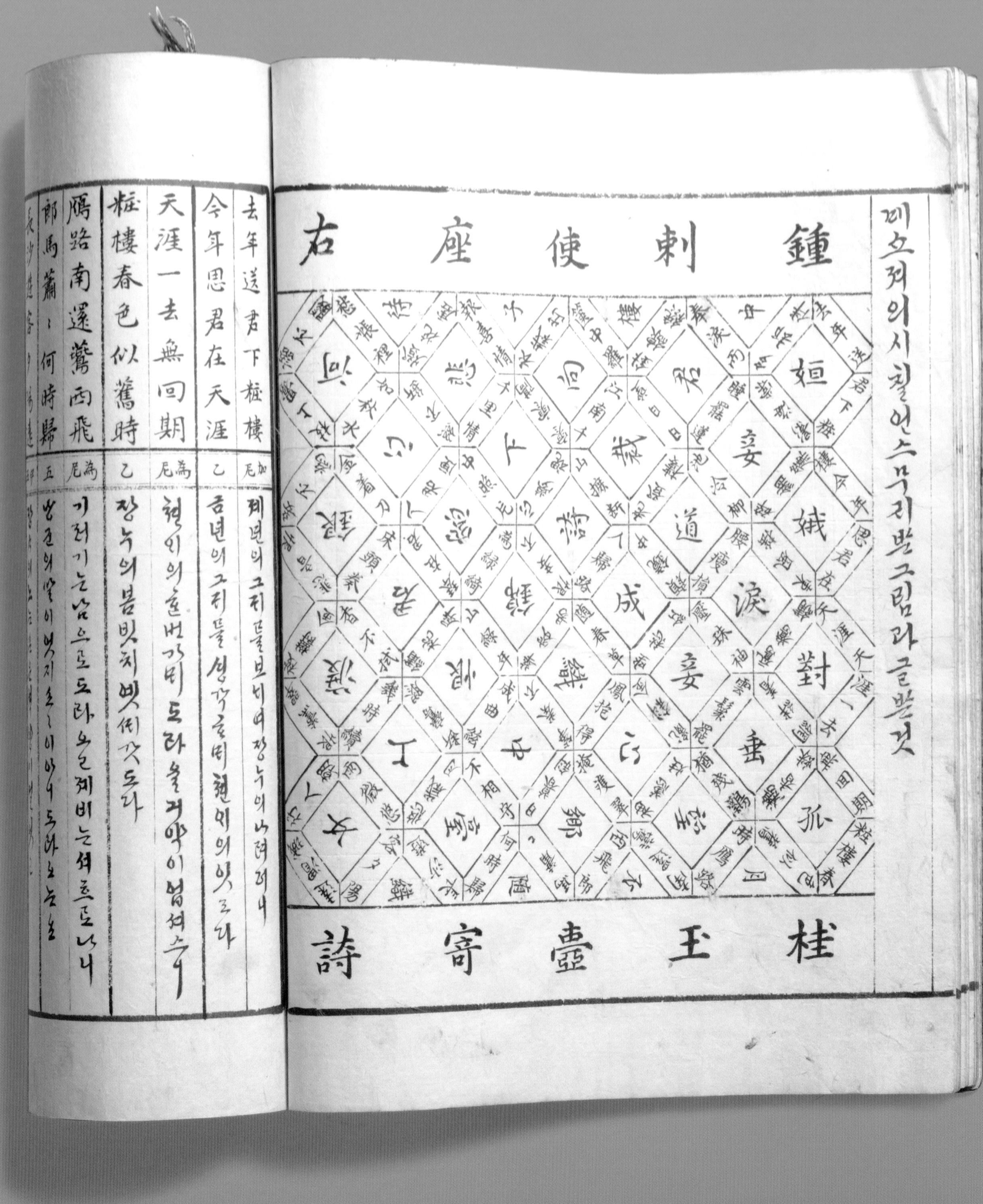

右 座 使 刺 鍾

詩 寄 壺 玉 桂

去年送君下糚樓
今年思君在天涯
天涯一去無回期
糚樓春色似舊時
鴈路南還驚雨飛
郎馬蕭蕭何時歸
長沙遠客...

Hwanghwa chip. Woodblock. Ca. 1773.

At the completion of a mission, the poems exchanged between Chinese emissaries and their Korean hosts were often collected and printed. Unsurprisingly, most of the contents are conventional in form. The collection dating to 1606, which includes palindromes and "Dongpo verse," is an exception. Named after the Song dynasty literatus Su Shi, also known as Su Dongpo, each verse contains only a fraction of the characters it should but is written in such a way as to suggest the missing text. In this detail, for instance, the first character on the right, "wall," is elongated, and the components of the character below, "gradually," are too far apart: "The Great Wall is gradually more distant."

Haedong kayo, EDITED BY KIM SU-JANG. MANUSCRIPT. UNDATED.

Some forms of verse were enjoyed at all levels of Korean society. The vernacular lyrics known as sijo *were transmitted through performance for centuries before professional singers began to compile collections for their own reference. Skilled singers improvised in performance, creating new lyrics or reworking old ones. This anthology,* Songs from East of the Sea, *was compiled by the professional Kim Su-jang, active between the late seventeenth and early eighteenth centuries.*

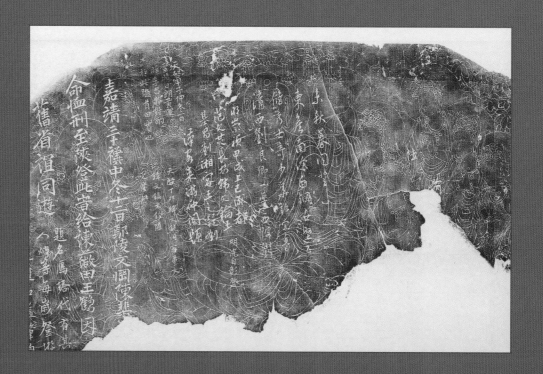

Graffiti

Pleasure is not a notion generally associated with the civil service examinations of imperial China. Yet in a society that offered its educated elite few opportunities to earn a livelihood outside the government and that encouraged state service, especially service that would bring honor to one's family, success at the examinations was cause for celebration. Passage meant a place in the bureaucracy; top graduates were assured of the choicest positions.

During the Tang dynasty, examinees who made the grade celebrated in the Xingyuan, Apricot Park, in the southeast quarter of the capital of Chang'an (present-day Xi'an). One year—sources differ as to exactly when—the candidates wandered over to a nearby temple, Ci'en si, and wrote their names on the walls of a pagoda on the temple grounds, Dayan ta, the Big Wild Goose Pagoda.

The pagoda and the temple were closely associated with the monk Xuanzang, who journeyed to India in the seventh century in search of scriptures. Returning to Chang'an more than fifteen years after he had set out and bringing with him over 650 sutras in addition to images and relics, Xuanzang set about the task of translating the texts into Chinese. Much of this work was carried out at Ci'en si, at the invitation of the emperor. The Big Wild Goose Pagoda was built for Xuanzang under imperial auspices and in a style the monk had seen in India. It remained a site of particular interest long after Chang'an lost its preeminence with the fall of the Tang, in 907.

The custom of autographing the pagoda was repeated over the years and amplified. Where the Tang celebrants had been content with writing their names on the pagoda's walls with brush and ink, later visitors had theirs carved into the Tang stone reliefs set into the pagoda's lintels. Where Tang officials are known to have updated their inscriptions on advancement by adding a single character or overwriting in red, the lintels show that some later visitors added entirely new inscriptions with subsequent visits. Where tradition tells us that only successful exam candidates inscribed their names on the pagoda's walls during the Tang, many who left their marks on the pagoda's reliefs in later eras identify themselves simply as appreciative tourists.

Foreign Exchange

Dutch learning

In the first half of the seventeenth century, the Japanese shogunate issued a series of edicts that effectively isolated the island empire. Japanese subjects and sea vessels were to travel abroad only under license, Portuguese and Spaniards were expelled from Japan, and all other foreign residents—that is, all affiliates of the Dutch East India Company—were restricted to the artificial island of Dejima, in Nagasaki Bay. Historians have characterized the move as xenophobic, anti-Christian, an attempt to suppress outlying daimyo who, with the power lent them through trade-wealth or the manipulation of Christian converts, might threaten the supremacy of the Tokugawa shogunate. Whatever their object, the proscriptions resulted in Nagasaki's becoming the center of "Dutch" or Western learning in seclusionist Japan, learning that was initially introduced primarily through medicine.

The Dutch East India physicians engaged in more than ministration. From the first years of the confinement to Dejima, Company doctors (who might be Dutch, German, or Swedish) offered instruction in Western medical theory and practice. Some of their pupils were their own Japanese interpreters; others were physicians trained in traditional Japanese medicine. These pupils went on to practice or to teach others what they had learned on Dejima; they wrote treatises on Dutch medicine; they made their own translations of the European medical texts that Company doctors had brought with them to Japan.

[PAGE 140 AND ABOVE]

KAITAI SHINSHO, BY JOHANN ADAM
KULMUS, TRANSLATED BY SUGITA
GENPAKU. WOODBLOCK. 1774.

*In Sugita's frontispiece, two grampuses,
symbols of the city of Nagoya, replace
Valverde's coat of arms; the name of
Sugita's private library replaces that of
Valverde's publisher; and on the frieze,
"Translated from the Dutch" replaces the
Biblical inscription "The Lord Is My
Helper." The use of the Valverde Adam
and Eve was a daring act at a time
when secret Christians were still being
persecuted in Tokugawa Japan, a fact
well known to Sugita.*

One of these translations was Sugita Genpaku's *Kaitai shinsho*. Sugita
was a traditionally trained physician with some knowledge of Western
medicine and curiosity enough to acquire the Dutch translation of
Johann Adam Kulmus's *Anatomische Tabellen*. Struck by the divergence
between Eastern and Western notions of anatomy he saw in the *Tabellen*'s
illustrations, Sugita resolved the difference empirically, by attending
a postmortem.

Dissection was practiced at that time, if not fully accepted. The postmortem Sugita observed ultimately lent respectability to the exercise,
however, for it revealed that Kulmus's illustrations accurately reflected
the appearance and position of the organs and viscera; that in turn led
to the publication of the first Japanese translation of a Western anatomy,
Sugita's translation of Kulmus.

Sugita worked on the translation with Maeno Ryōtaku and three other
colleagues over three years. The finished work, *Kaitai shinsho, A New
Anatomy*, contained woodblock reproductions of illustrations in the
Dutch translation of the *Tabellen*. The frontispiece of the atlas volume
was borrowed from Valverde's *Vivae imagines partium corporis humani*,
probably in Christopher Plantin's Antwerp edition.

Kaitai shinsho inspired a wave of interest in dissection and Dutch medicine, as well as in the rational approach they exemplified. More broadly,
Kaitai shinsho has been credited with exciting Japanese interest in the
West's study of other branches of science, including natural history,
astronomy, and mathematics.

NAGASAKI SAIKEN NO ZU. COLOR WOODBLOCK. 1851.

Nagasaki and Nagasaki Bay. The curved trapezoid just below the masted ship flying colors but no sails is where the Dutch East India Company was confined. The almost-square island, Shinchi-machi, is where Chinese traders were quartered.

RANGAKU KAITEI, BY ŌTSUKI
GENTAKU. WOODBLOCK. 1788.

*The first, and for decades the leading,
school of Dutch learning in Japan was
the Shirandō Juku, founded by a student
of Sugita's and Maeno's, Ōtsuki Shigetada,
who later took the name Gentaku—an
amalgam of Sugita's and Maeno's given
names—to express his admiration for his
teachers. Among his many writings was*
Rangaku kaitei, *the first Japanese work
devoted to the study of Dutch and Dutch
learning. Less than twenty years previous
to* Rangaku kaitei's *initial publication,
the printing blocks of another work had
been destroyed for including the Dutch
alphabet.*

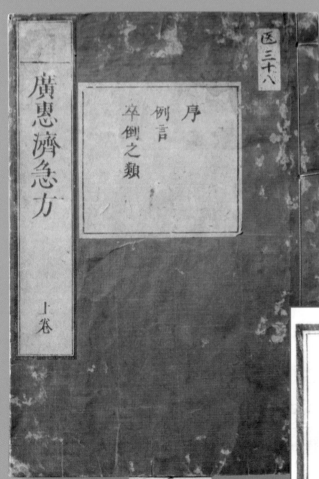

Kōkei saikyūhō, by Taki Motonori, edited by Taki Motoyasu. Woodblock. 1790.

The introduction of Western medicine did not immediately end the dominance of traditional Chinese medicine as practiced in Japan. Shortly after the publication of Kaitai shinsho, *the shogun commanded court physician Taki Motonori to compile a first-aid manual for general distribution. The diagnoses and remedies in the manual reflected the Chinese theories of medicine Taki had been trained in. Curiously, one of the manual's illustrations was later used in Arturo Castiglioni's* Storia della medicina. *Here, how to find the acupuncture and moxibustion point* chūkūn.

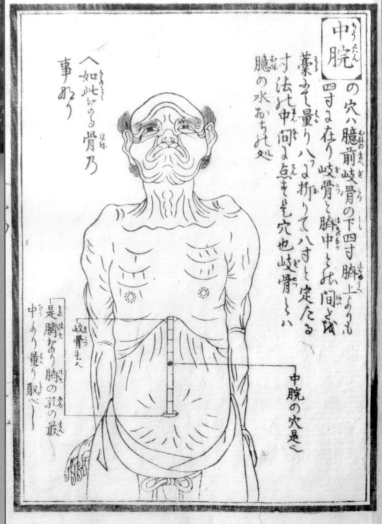

Sakhalin ethnography

It was not until 1787 that Europe discovered through the explorations of Jean-François de Galaup, comte de la Pérouse, that the northernmost tip of Japan was separated from Sakhalin by a channel of water now called La Pérouse Strait. And it was not until 1809 that Japan, and later Europe, discovered through the explorations of Mamiya Rinzō, son of a barrel maker, that Sakhalin was an island, separated from the mainland of the Asian continent by a channel of water now called Mamiya Strait, or Tatar Strait.

At the frontiers of Japan, Russia, and the Manchurian lands of the Qing empire, Sakhalin was ideally situated for controversy. The Japanese shogunate, realizing it must have a better understanding of the lands beyond its northern borders, sent Mamiya first in 1808 and again in 1808–9 to settle the question of Sakhalin's insularity. Mamiya had studied under the cartographer Inō Tadataka and had originally been sent to Ezo (modern Hokkaido) as a surveyor. Happily, his observations of Sakhalin extended beyond the topographical to the economic, anthropological, and ethnographical.

Kita Ezo zusetsu, An Illustrated Account of the Regions North of Ezo, is based on unpublished reports Mamiya delivered to the shogunate on returning from his Sakhalin expeditions. These were written with the aid of Hata Sadakado, who recorded and edited Mamiya's oral account, which Mamiya based on his written journals; they were supplemented with Mamiya's own sketches and maps.

Mamiya's powers of observation, which have proven keen enough to satisfy even modern anthropologists, were fully appreciated during his lifetime. In Japan, the shogunate had Mamiya carry out further intelligence-gathering missions. In Europe, Philipp Franz von Siebold publicized Mamiya's discovery of Sakhalin's insularity. Siebold also based the pages concerning Sakhalin in his own account of Japan, *Nippon*, directly on Mamiya.

Siebold first learned of Sakhalin's insularity in 1826, while serving as physician to the Dutch East India Company in Japan. During that time he also obtained a copy of a map of Japan's coastline based on surveys carried out by Inō Tadataka. Cartographically detailed and scientifically accurate, Inō's map was considered a state secret for what it could reveal about Japan's defenses and vulnerabilities. Takahashi Kageyasu, keeper of the map, nevertheless offered a copy of it to Siebold in the spirit of scientific exchange—a gesture that was deemed an act of treason by the Japanese officials who found the map among Siebold's possessions. Siebold was thereupon expelled from Japan, Takahashi died in prison, and Mamiya was ostracized by his colleagues for the remainder of his life, widely suspected of having informed on the cartographer and the physician.

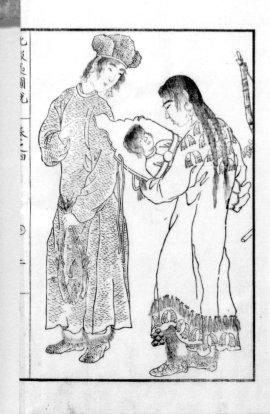 

KITA EZO ZUSETSU, BY MAMIYA
RINZŌ AND HATA SADAKADO,
ILLUSTRATED BY HASHIMOTO
GYOKURANSAI (SADAHIDE).
WOODBLOCK. 1855.

*Mamiya identified three main ethnic
groups among the inhabitants of Sakhalin.
Many of the attributes of the Sumeren-
kuru, or Gilyaks, described by Mamiya
can be identified here: the abundant hair
and the way in which it is dressed; the
heavy eyebrows; both sexes' fondness for
earrings; boots and leggings of animal or
fish skin. During the day, the board to
which the toddler is strapped served as
a sort of vertical cradle, suspended by the
thongs that here hang loose. Dogs were
used for fishing, hunting, and transporting
goods, and were treated with affection
in return.*

*This woodblock also alludes to the bear
sacrifice of the Ainu, Gilyaks, and other
tribes of northeastern Asia, who revered
the animal as a deity or divine messenger.
In a ritual sequence common to many
traditions, the bear, obtained as a cub,
was shown all the care shown a human
baby, even suckled, until it grew too
large. Sacrifice and ritual consumption
took place after the bear reached its
maturity. Modern anthropologists
characterize the rite as an opportunity
to host a divinity, partake of its strength
and virtue, and, through death, release
its soul to return to its proper home.*

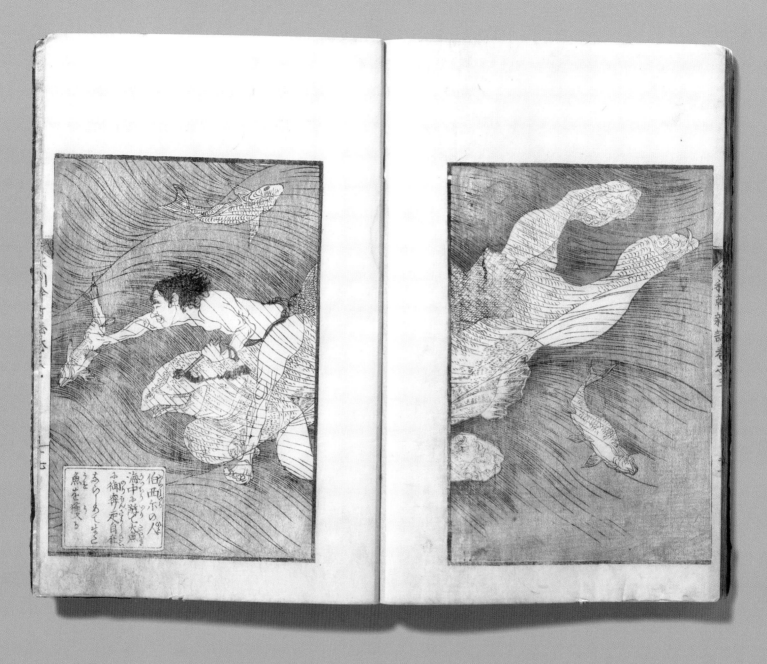

MERIKEN SHINSHI, BY TSURUMINE SHIGENOBU, ILLUSTRATED BY
GYOKURANSAI SADAHIDE (SADAHIDE). WOODBLOCK. 1855.

*From the mid-nineteenth century on, the Japanese reading public demonstrated an
unprecedented interest in travel literature, an interest undoubtedly quickened by
Commodore Matthew Perry's visit to Japan in 1853 but by no means wholly
generated by it. The book in which this illustration appears,* A New Account of
the Americas, *was written specifically to satisfy younger readers' curiosity about
other lands. Here, underwater fishing off Brazil.*

ENGINEERING IN TRANSLATION

In 1789, King Chŏngjo had the tomb of his father, Prince Sado, moved to Hwasŏng, also known as Suwŏn. He intended that the capital, then at Seoul, would follow. Chŏngjo's public purpose was to honor his father: much ceremony accompanied the reinterment, and the new buildings that would be raised to house the central government would be viewed by many as a shrine to the late prince. Historians agree that Chŏngjo had another, more immediate purpose: to remove himself from the factional struggles that had taken root in Seoul and were threatening the continued authority of the dynasty. Adopting his predecessor's policy of appointing officials impartially, Chŏngjo ordered a member of the minority faction, Chŏng Yag-yong, to prepare construction plans for the new capital.

Chŏng was more than a political outsider. He had been reared in an atmosphere of intellectual open-mindedness and educated in a philosophical tradition that advocated "practical learning" over abstract speculation. His planning for the construction of Hwasŏng reflected this. Where tradition would have separated defense works from city walls, Chŏng combined the two, incorporating battlements, beacons, observation and command posts into the walls enclosing Hwasŏng. He also introduced machinery, such as pulleys and cranes, to assist with construction. The machinery especially pleased the throne, since it saved considerable expense.

The machines were based on models and principles presented in *Qiqi tushuo, Illustrated Discourses on Miraculous Machines*, a collaboration between the Jesuit missionary Johann Schreck and the Chinese scholar-official Wang Zheng. *Qiqi tushuo* opened with a discussion of the mathematics underlying the mechanics, and concluded with illustrated descriptions of particular machines. The machines were selected from European sources ranging from Vitruvius to Jacques Besson. Schreck translated the Western text into colloquial Chinese; Wang distilled it into the classical Chinese more appropriate for print. The illustrations included were based on those in the Jesuit's books.

Chŏng's success and the king's favor stirred jealousy among members of the entrenched faction. Even within his own faction, Chŏng's introduction of Western ideas raised suspicion. When it was discovered that members of his family had converted to Catholicism, rumor accused Chŏng of sedition. With the death of Chŏngjo in 1800, charges were pressed, and while they were ultimately withdrawn, Chŏng never regained the position or influence he once had. Nor did he again have the chance to apply newly acquired ideas to the practice of architecture and construction.

Much of the Hwasŏng's walls and fortifications were destroyed in the first half of the twentieth century, during Japan's colonization of Korea and later during the Korean War. The government began reconstruction and restoration of the site in 1964. In 1997, Unesco named Hwasŏng Fortress a world heritage site, noting especially its use of the most advanced features of early modern military architecture from both East and West.

Hwasŏng sŏngyok ŭigwe.
METAL MOVABLE TYPE WITH
WOODBLOCK. 1800.

*On the order of King Chŏngjo, Hwasŏng
sŏngyok ŭigwe, documenting the
construction of Hwasŏng's walls and fortifications, was printed in an extremely
limited issue. Two hundred years later,
the book proved an invaluable asset to
the work of restoration and reconstruction.
On the right, an interior view of a
crossbowmen's tower. European military
architects preferred towers with curved
perimeters rather than squared corners,
which rendered the structures more
vulnerable when bombarded or rammed.*

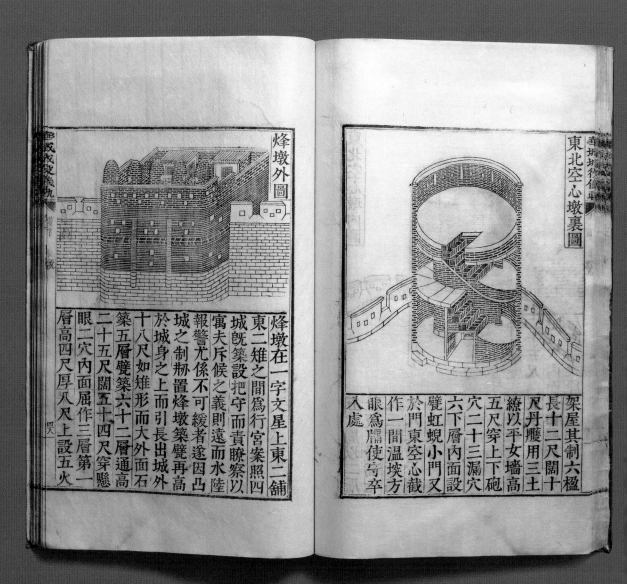

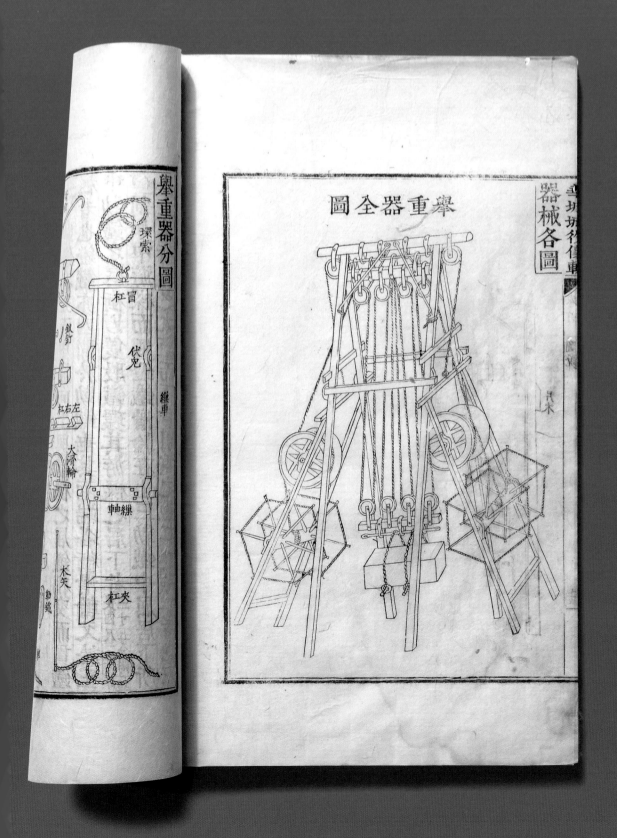

Hwasŏng sŏngyok ŭigwe.
METAL MOVABLE TYPE WITH
WOODBLOCK, 1800.

*Hwasŏng was exceptional in being built
on both hilly and flat land, a measure that
increased defensive effectiveness but made
construction more difficult. Chŏng
compared using machines such as this
to hoist heavy loads to "using a heavy
butcher knife to cut up a skinny chicken."*

Missionary of science

Unlike the Jesuits, who brought the principles of Western science to Ming China hoping to attract converts by engaging their intellects, John Fryer devoted himself to the gospel of science and engineering only after surrendering his role as missionary.

Raised in the southeast of England, the son of a poor clergyman, Fryer traveled to Asia under the auspices of the Church Missionary Society in the early 1860s. He parted ways with the society seven years later, convinced that the promotion of science, not the conversion of souls, was crucial to China's welfare.

This brought Fryer, in 1868, to the Jiangnan Arsenal in Shanghai. Arsenal officials had established a translation office realizing that their ability to manufacture armaments would remain limited as long as the principles underlying the arms' invention remained a mystery. Fryer's job was to translate Western works in the applied, natural, and military sciences. He worked as the Jesuits had, with a scholar-official who polished his rough oral translations into classical Chinese. The method ensured translations that were faithful, elegant, and fairly quickly completed.

In the coming years, Fryer and his Chinese colleagues translated over a hundred Western works. The achievement is formidable when the problems involved in translation at that time are considered. There were no words, for example, for most of the elements in the periodic table. To transcribe the sounds of the Western terms would have resulted in unwieldy and uninformative strings of characters. To create new Chinese characters for the terms would have been to risk censure from all sides, especially from philologists and xenophobes. This is nevertheless what Fryer and his chief collaborator, Xu Shou, ultimately decided to do.

What began as a job became a mission. When Fryer discovered that the translations were not making the impact he would have liked, he attempted a more popular approach to science, establishing a lecture series, a reading room, essay contests, and, most notably, the publication of *Gezhi huibian, The Chinese Scientific Magazine*. Even after returning to the West in 1896, to found what would later become the Department of East Asian Languages and Cultures at the University of California at Berkeley, Fryer continued the work he had started in Shanghai.

Some modern historians dismiss Fryer's efforts as futile. Others conclude that his influence has proven significant, if diffuse. His collaborators continued to publish translations and some entered academics, paving the way for the induction of Western science into the Chinese curriculum. Fryer and Xu's translation of *Wells's Principles and Applications of Chemistry, Huaxue jianyuan*, is commonly considered "the most influential textbook on chemistry in nineteenth-century China." And the characters Fryer and Xu created can be found in the back of any Chinese dictionary that includes a periodic table.

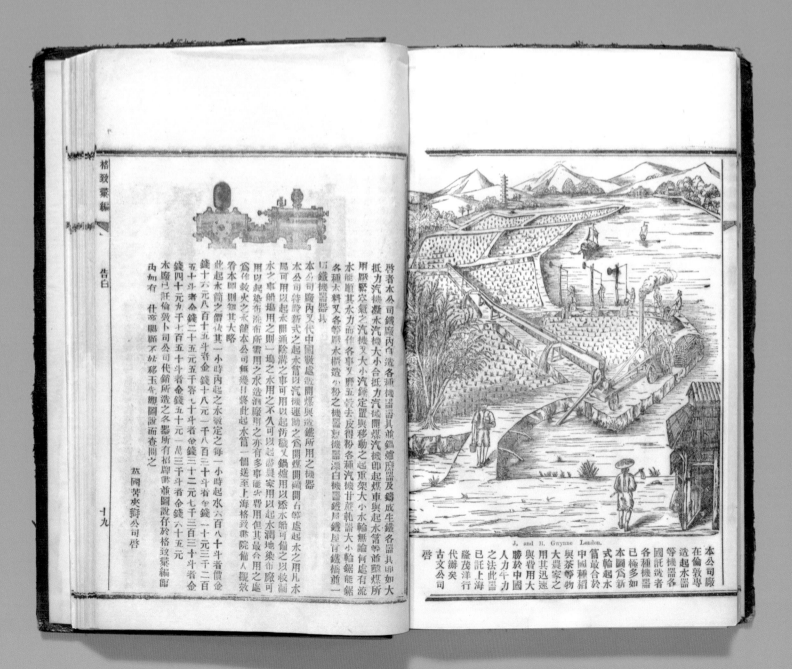

GEZHI HUIBIAN. 1876.

Most of the illustrations in Fryer's Chinese Scientific Magazine *were reprinted from British and American journals. This illustration, demonstrating the efficiency of J. and H. Gwynne's steam-powered pumps, clearly was not. While advertisements printed in the magazine helped fund publication, they were also intended to spread awareness of Western technology.*

下墈

敝魚子山

和尚山

敝魚子門

杭塢山烽墩

烏峰山烽墩

馬鞍山烽墩

三江港

三江所

合龍山隘

三江巡司

敝風岱隘

錢塘江

白洋巡司

蓬萊驛

西興驛

蕭山縣

Mapping Land and Sea

Coastal defense

Japanese pirates plagued the China coast in the mid-sixteenth century, or so it was believed. When a geographer concerned with the empire's coastal defenses managed to interview captured Japanese pirates, he learned that in fact they were working under the direction of local Chinese, who far outnumbered them. The geographer, Zheng Ruozeng, had already completed an atlas of maritime China. At the time he interviewed the pirates he was compiling a handbook intended to aid government officials forced to deal with the pirates' activities. Zheng revealed the true nature of the situation in that handbook, *Chouhai tubian*, or *Illustrated Discourses on Coastal Defense*.

Although pirates had been visiting the Korean and Chinese seaboards for two centuries, at the time Zheng was compiling *Chouhai tubian* the situation was both more egregious and more complex than it had ever been. An interdiction on maritime trade had led to illicit commerce between Chinese merchants and Asian, Southeast Asian, and possibly Portuguese traders. Unable to pay their debts to the traders, the merchants called on local authorities to stop the traders, who turned to piracy to recoup their losses. In place of smuggling and occasional coastal raids, there was determined incursion and pillaging. Inland, as well as on the coast, towns and cities were attacked, besieged, and captured, and lives were lost.

Hu Zongxian is the military official generally credited with suppressing the pirates. In spite of this, Hu became the target of a political attack and was arrested only a year after his celebrated victory.

Chouhai tubian, attributed
to Hu Zongxian, by Zheng
Ruozeng. Woodblock. 1624.

*The Qiantang River, to the left, allowed
the pirates to penetrate inland to Hangzhou, which they raided on more than one
occasion. Oriented to the east, this map
shows the signal towers situated along
the coast. In times of emergency, beacon
fires were set in the towers. Because the
towers were within sight of one another,
the alarm traveled as quickly as the fires
could be set.*

While he was awaiting trial, former subordinates wrote highly favorable accounts of Hu's victory, probably hoping to influence the powers in Beijing. Some of these accounts are included in *Chouhai tubian*. Forgiven by the emperor in 1563, Hu was again arrested on a pretext in 1565 and died in jail before any adjudication was reached.

Zheng Ruozeng had completed *Chouhai tubian* under Hu's sponsorship in 1564; two editions naming Zheng as author were issued before the end of the century. In 1624, Hu's grandsons and great grandson published another edition, this one naming Hu Zongxian as author and with any text suggesting otherwise altered or excised. This act of intellectual piracy was possibly inspired by a desire to rehabilitate Hu Zongxian's reputation. Decades later, descendants of Zheng Ruozeng responded with their own edition, restoring Zheng as author. Confusion over the attribution none-theless continued, even in scholarly and bibliographical circles, well into the Qing dynasty.

Unlike its authorship, the contribution *Chouhai tubian* made to China's defenses was never in question. Historically, China's northern frontier had been seen as its most vulnerable spot, and its western frontiers as a constant source of trouble. Geographers and officials concerned with defense had accordingly concentrated on these areas. *Chouhai tubian* demonstrated that the seaboard could not be ignored.

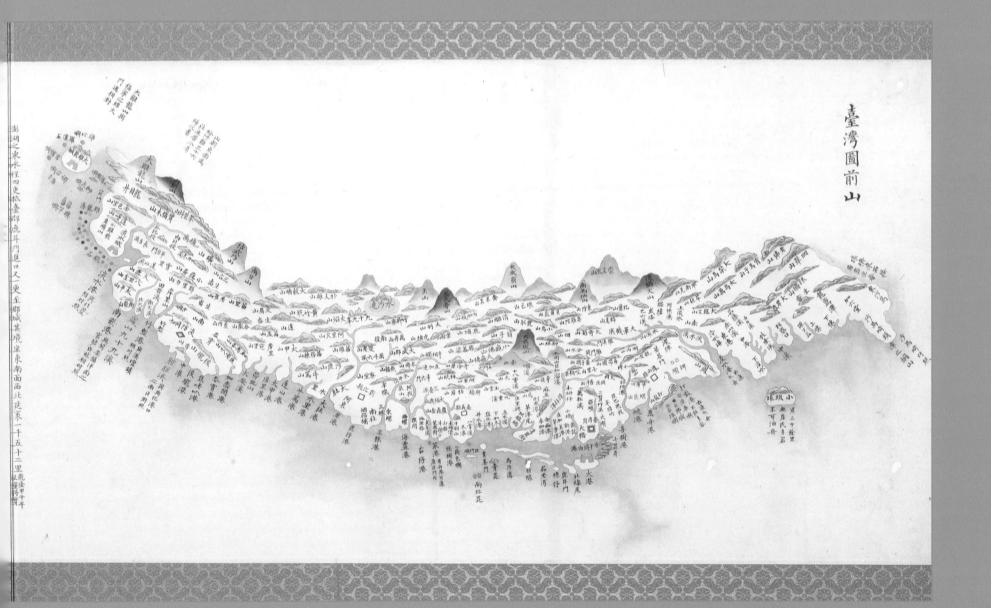

臺灣圖前山

[*QISHENG YANHAI TU*]. HANDSCROLL, INK AND COLOR ON PAPER.
AFTER 1787.

*Coastal defense continued to be of concern into the Qing dynasty. This detail is taken
from a handscroll of the eastern seaboard of China, identifying all islands and inlets
and occasionally noting areas known to be pirates' anchorages. Here, the western coast
of Taiwan from Jiayi to Gaoxiong. The ruins of Fort Zeelandia can be seen on the
peninsula opposite what is now Tainan. The Dutch colonized Taiwan from 1624
to 1662.*

TAEDONG YŎJIDO, BY KIM CHŎNG-HO.
WOODBLOCK. 1861

Kaesŏng, or Kaegyŏng, was the capital of
Koryŏ when the Khitan marched on the city
and seized it in response to the murder of
their vassal, King Mokchong, in the eleventh
century. The assault led to the printing of the
first Korean Buddhist canon.

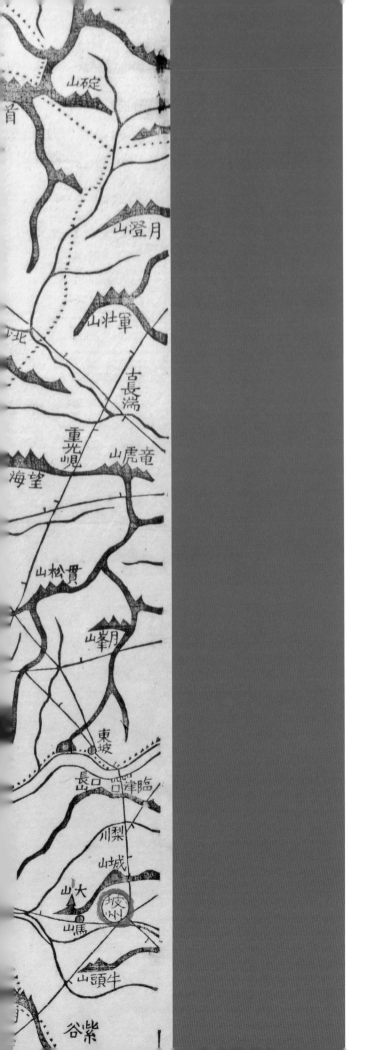

Invasion

Between the sixth century and the seventeenth, Korea was invaded by the Chinese, the Khitan, the Mongols, the Japanese, and the Manchus. Defense was a constant concern, and the government compiled and collected maps that would assist with it. Because these maps would also assist with invasion, they were not published; nor was the information they contained readily shared. The government regarded maps as critical to national security and continued to do so even after the start of commercial map publication.

The first half of the nineteenth century brought new threats to Korea's borders. The Japanese were once again eying Korea with interest. With the Opium Wars, Britain and France demonstrated the strength of the Western powers as well as their determination to wring profit from Asia. French, British, Russian, and American ships were sighted off Korea's coasts. And inside Korea, French missionaries challenging the hegemony of Neo-Confucianism were seen by some as enemy agents. In 1861, Kim Chŏng-ho, a printer and independent cartographer, responded to the threat by compiling and publishing his *Taedong yŏjido, Maps of the Lands of the Great East.*

Kim had earlier compiled an atlas of Korea, *Ch'ŏnggudo,* which modern scholars have praised for its detail, comprehensiveness, and ease of use. In compiling *Taedong yŏjido* Kim used not only updated data but a clearer drafting style and a format that made the maps even easier to read than *Ch'ŏnggudo*'s. He also omitted material that was irrelevant to military preparation and defense.

Tradition holds that Kim Chŏng-ho was imprisoned on presenting *Taedong yŏjido* to the throne and that the blocks used to print it were confiscated and destroyed. The charge was breaching national security by publishing the maps. Modern scholars are skeptical of the story, though so little is known of Kim's life that it is hard to refute. Copies of *Taedong yŏjido* are scarce today, yet there is evidence that a second printing, or perhaps a second edition, was issued in 1864, three years after its first publication. Kim's concern for Korea's security was justified soon after: within a decade of *Taedong yŏjido*'s publication, Korea had clashed with France and the United States, and within fifty years it had become a colony of Japan.

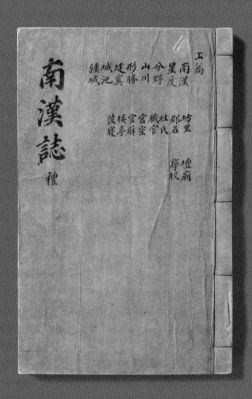

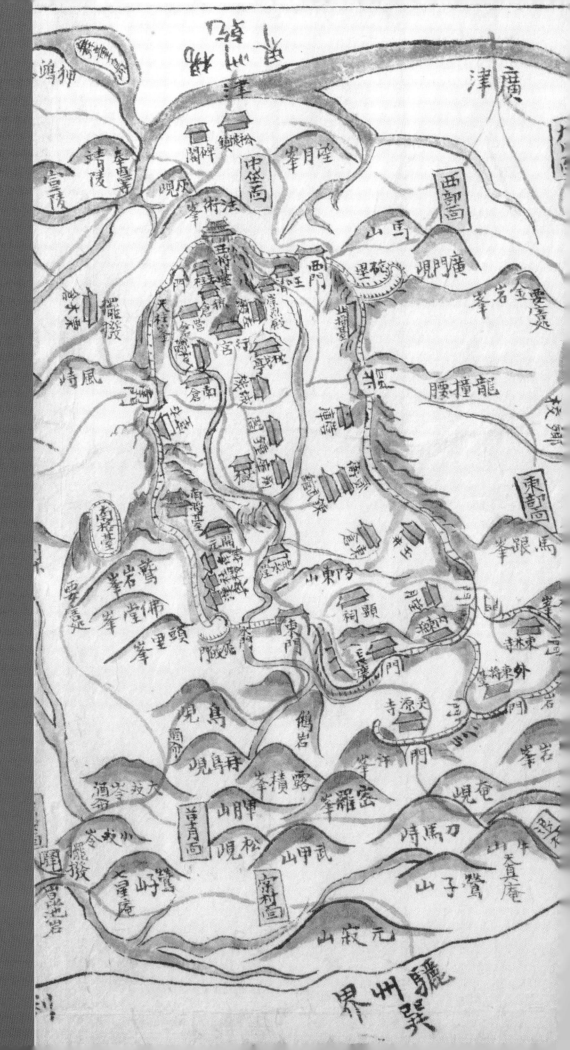

Chungjŏng Namhanji, by Hong Kyŏng-mo. Ink and color on paper. Undated.

Namhansansŏng was one of three fortresses built as redoubts for the Korean court at Seoul. King Injo fled here when the Manchus invaded, in 1636, and laid siege to the stronghold. Injo is said to have stayed in the Sŏjang-dae, the two-storied pavilion between the west and south gates (the second story was added in 1751). Just inside the east gate is the Hyŏn-sa, or Hyŏnjŏl-sa, a memorial to the Korean officials who urged King Injo not to yield to the Manchus and who were killed by their conquerors when he did.

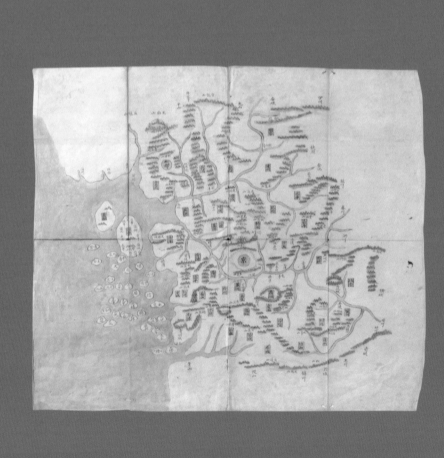

CH'ŎNGGU YŎRAM. INK AND COLOR ON PAPER. 18TH CENTURY.

Located at the mouth of the Han River, which winds around Seoul's southern and western flanks, Kanghwa Island was a natural refuge for the court in flight. It was also a natural target for enemy forces. In the seventeenth century, the Manchus took the island, along with members of the royal family who had fled there. Five years after the publication of Taedong yŏjido, *the French attacked the island, and five years after that the Americans attacked in retaliation for the mistreatment of French and American nationals.*

[OPPOSITE PAGE]

DAI NIHON DŌCHŪ KŌTEI SAIKENKI,
BY SUIGASHI (TORIKAI DŌSAI).
COLOR WOODBLOCK. 1770.

This diagrammatic route map, measuring 644 centimeters long, was sufficient to guide the traveler as far west Korea and as far north as Hokkaido. Identified along the way are routes, towns, temples, and shrines. Daimyo's seats are marked by name and crest, with notes concerning income and management. The map's opening text provides information on distances to foreign parts, including Holland, and a checklist of necessities for the road.

COMMERCIAL MAP MAKING

Japan's central government began mapping the empire in the seventh century. The mapping was carried out over the succeeding eras by local government offices, daimyo, or teams of surveyors sent out from the capital. It was always grounded in the government's desire to understand its boundaries and who held how much land.

By the seventeenth century, government maps were being drawn up according to a fixed standard and scale, and based on recently conducted surveys. Toward the middle of that century, the state of the nation was stable, the economy was growing. The government no longer felt it had to withhold the information the maps could yield, and non-official travelers had an unprecedented need for it. Commercial map publishers responded to that need by joining the skills of cartographers or *ukiyo-e* artists with information that was readily available.

The information varied, naturally, according to the commercially published map's intended use and audience. A provincial map would indicate trunk roads and towns, historic sites or local products. A map of Edo might note daimyo's residences and their crests. A map of Kyoto might use different colors to distinguish commoners' residences from peers'. There were city maps devoted to recording damage done by fires or earthquakes. There were pilgrimage maps that made no attempt to depict the topography or to provide any information not directly related to temples and shrines, while others provided information more pertinent to the tourist than the religious devotee.

Cartographical accuracy varied as well. Finding that precision was not enough to sell maps, *ukiyo-e* artists added vignettes and their own palettes to the maps. Some of these bear censors' seals indicating official permission to be published as decorative prints. They sold well, frequently better than maps more cartographically reliable, stimulating not only sales but the public's interest in maps and the world they described.

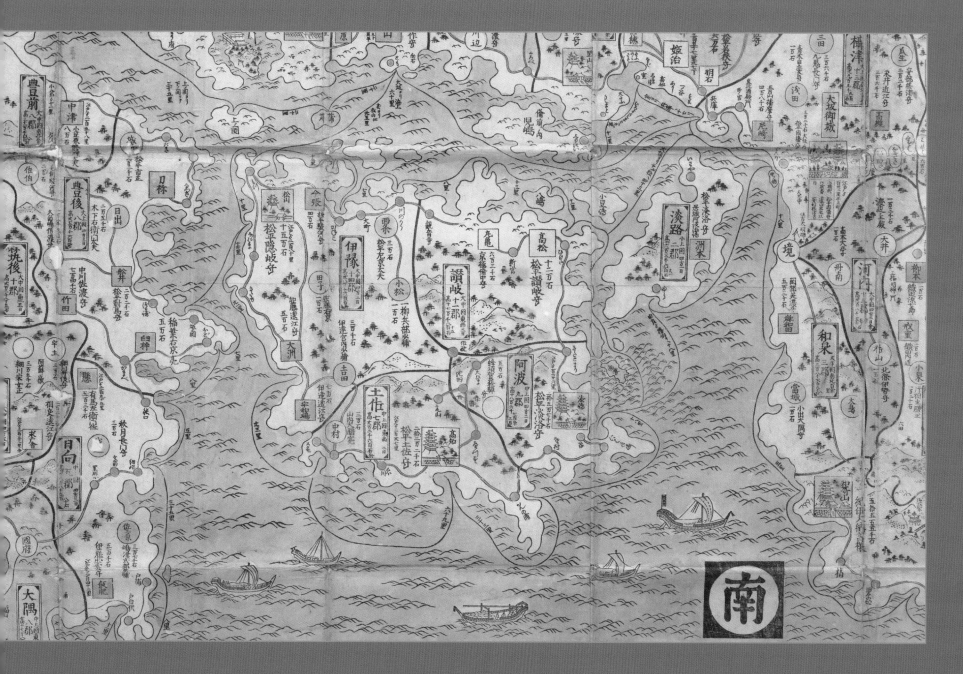

NIHON KAISAN CHŌRIKUZU ZU, BY ISHIKAWA RYŪSEN. WOODBLOCK WITH
HAND-COLORING. 1694.

The prominence given the name of the mapmaker, ukiyo-e *artist Ishikawa Ryūsen,*
suggests that this map's success owed as much to its aesthetic appeal as to its carto-
graphic qualities. In the century following its first publication, in 1687, Ryūsen's map
went through numerous editions and printings, spawned imitators, and informed
foreign cartographers. Adrien Reland is said to have used it in drafting his own
Imperium Japonicum *of 1715.*

Suruga no kuni Fujisan ezu. WOODBLOCK. 18TH CENTURY.

The Tōkaidō runs along the bottom of this map of Mount Fuji; the Murayama Sengen Shrine, marked by a torii gate, appears in the center. At the time this map was printed, Fuji was a pilgrimage site. The religious residing at the shrine assisted visitors in the rituals of pilgrimage and saw to it that no women ascended to the peak. By the time the restriction on women was abolished, in 1872, tourists far out- numbered pilgrims on the mountain. The path that runs by the shrine, the Murayama Kodō, was one of the main trails up Fuji until the early twentieth century.

WORLD VIEWS

Maps can reflect not only what we know of the world at a given time but what we want to know about it. Ming China had little interest in the Western world; the lessons the Jesuit Matteo Ricci tried to teach about cartography and the countries of Europe therefore made an initial impression on court literati but were ultimately dismissed. Ricci's map was given a different reception in Japan.

In spite of the Tokugawa shogunate's policy of isolation, there was curiosity and interest in the world beyond Japan's coasts, interest that the shogunate helped satisfy to a certain extent by excluding world maps from the ban on luxury goods imported from abroad. Chinese prints of Ricci's map that found their way to Japan were mounted onto screens, studied, copied. Ricci's served as the basis for the first world map printed in Japan, and for many subsequent oval-projection maps that added updated information culled from European traders' and missionaries' maps to the Ricci model. Even unrevised copies of Ricci's map continued to be printed and sold into the mid-nineteenth century.

European world maps employing stereographic projection did not enjoy the same popularity. One reason is that the hemispheric world map unambiguously portrayed the world as round; the notion was already familiar to scholars, but general acceptance would require rethinking the traditional Confucian cosmology still current in Japan. Another reason is that many Japanese still looked to China as the source of culture and learning, and many of them believed Ricci's map, which had been published under his Chinese name, to be Chinese in origin.

Those with much or little to lose were more receptive to new cartographic techniques and the cosmological schemes associated with them. Increasing contacts with foreign powers, especially Russia, led the shogunate to commission new maps based on the hemispheric model and incorporating the latest information, including Mamiya Rinzō's surveys of Sakhalin. And commoners, such as Hashimoto Sōkichi, published maps based on the newer models or wrote on related theories, like heliocentrism, that would challenge the Confucian world order and Japan's acceptance of it.

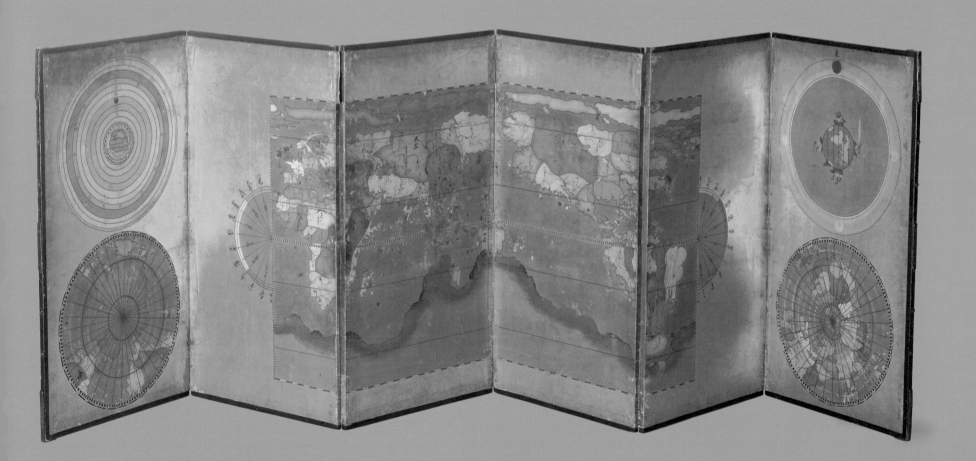

Sekaizu narabini Nihonzu byōbu. SCREEN, INK AND COLOR ON
PAPER. 1640.

*Screen maps were used primarily to furnish the homes of the wealthy and powerful
in sixteenth- and early seventeenth-century Japan. Based on European maps, the
Nanban, or "Southern Barbarian," screen maps were tailored to suit their function
and their owners' tastes, sacrificing geographical detail to aesthetic effect and often,
as here, placing the Pacific, and Japan, at the center of the world. Japan's size has
been increased in this map, to roughly a third of China's. The mix of known geography
with mythological (the Land of Women lies to the south of Japan) is not unusual
for the period.*

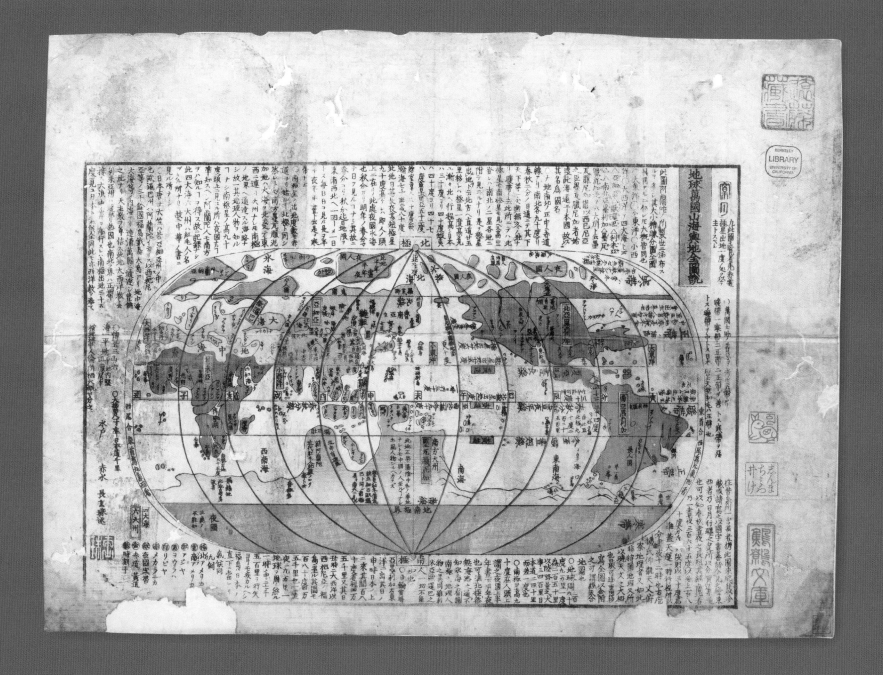

CHIKYŪ BANKOKU SANKAI YOCHI ZENZU, BY NAGAKUBO SEKISUI.
COLOR WOODBLOCK. 1850.

First published around 1785, Nagakubo Sekisui's world map was reprinted, and plagiarized, into the mid-nineteenth century. In his maps of Japan, Sekisui insisted on scientific accuracy; in his world maps, he employed a less stringent standard. The southern land mass Magellanica, combining Australia, New Guinea, and Tierra del Fuego, is a characteristic feature of Ricci-type maps.

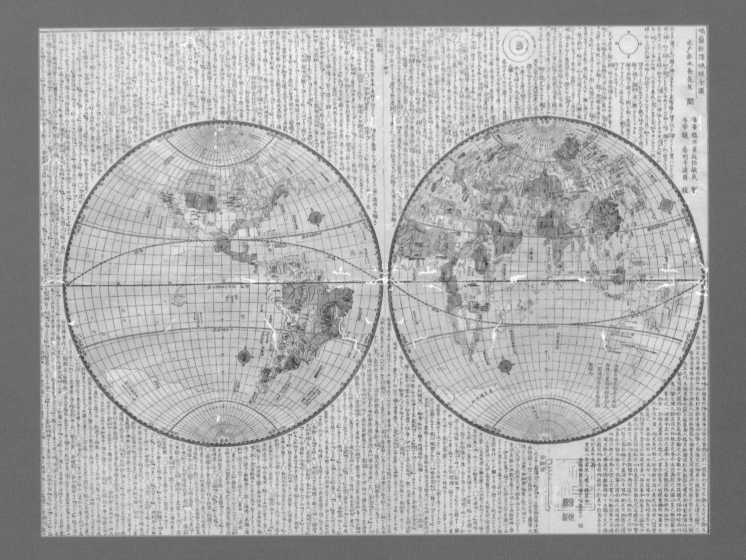

Oranda shinyaku chikyū zenzu, by Hashimoto Sōkichi.
Woodblock with hand-coloring. 1796.

European mapmakers continued to represent California as an island long after it
was proven and royally proclaimed, in 1747, to be contiguous with the continent. In
light of this, Hashimoto Sōkichi's representation of California in this map, published
in 1796, is not noteworthy; his use of stereographic projection is. Hashimoto was one
of the first Japanese mapmakers to abandon the oval projection used in Ricci's map
and its derivatives.

NIHON MEISHO NO E, BY KEISAI SHŌSHIN
(KITAO MASAYOSHI). COLOR WOODBLOCK. 1803.

*Admirers of early Japanese maps frequently remark on the
mapmakers' ability to include textual and pictographic detail
in panoramic vistas. Kitao Masayoshi's bird's-eye view of
Japan goes one step further, suggesting the world beyond
the archipelago, the horizon, and the limitations of scientific
cartographic technique.*

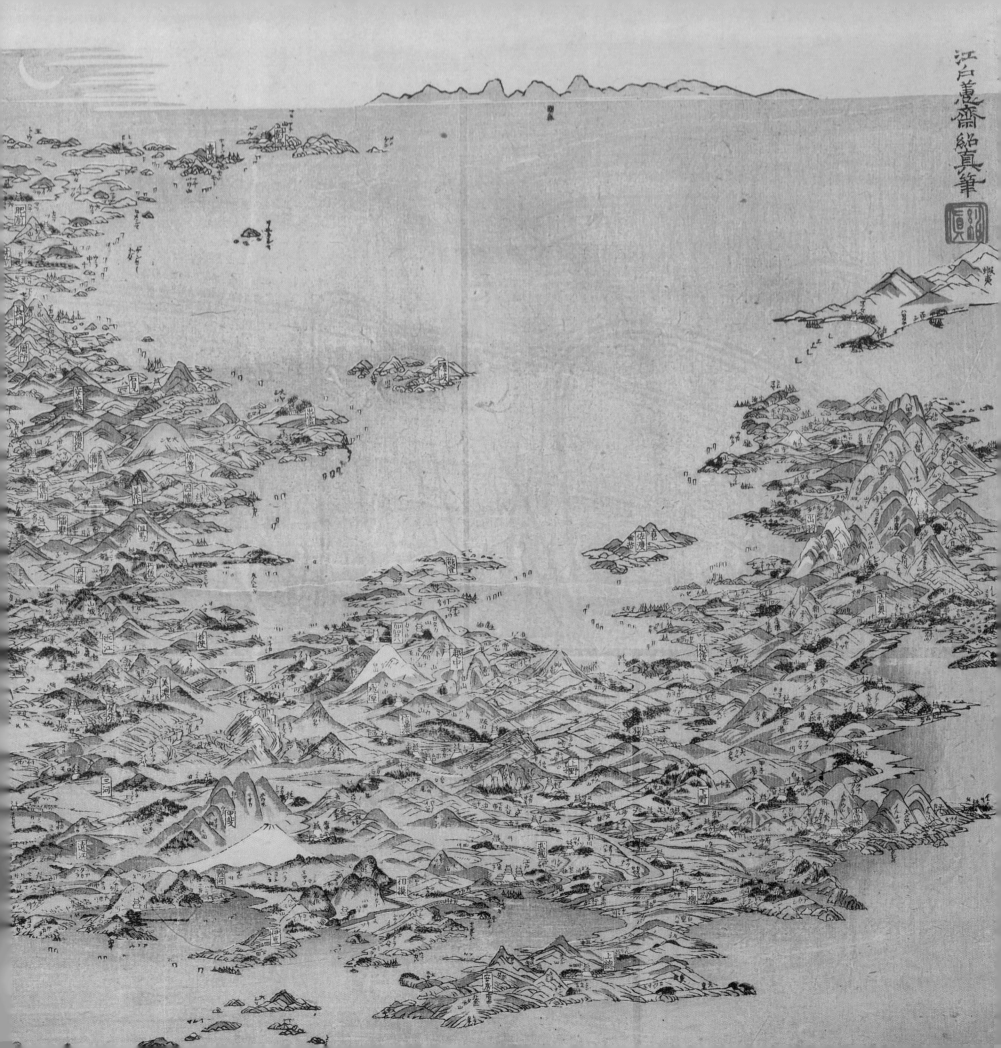

Works Featured

"Cheji tu" 車騎圖. 20th-cent. rubbing of relief dating to Eastern Han.

Cheng shi moyuan 程氏墨苑. Comp. Cheng Dayue 程大約. Woodblock. N.p.: Cheng shi Zilan tang, 1606.

Chikyū bankoku sankai yochi zenzu 地球万国山海輿地全図. By Nagakubo Sekisui 長久保赤水. Woodblock. N.p., 1850.

Ch'ŏnggu yoram 青岳要覽. Manuscript. 18th cent.

Ch'ŏnji p'arayang sinju kyŏng 天地八陽神咒經. Woodblock. Yangju, 1795–97.

Chouhai tubian 籌海圖編. Attr. Hu Zongxian 胡宗憲. By Zheng Ruozeng 鄭若曾. Woodblock. N.p.: Hu Weiji, 1624.

Chujŏng 酒政. Manuscript. N.d.

Chunch'ŏn kyech'ŏp 潘川禊帖. Rubbings, woodblock, manuscript. 1760?

Ch'unch'u Chwa ssi chŏn 春秋左氏傳. Ed. Yi Sŏ-gu 李書九 et al. Woodblock and movable type. N.p., 1797.

Chungjŏng Namhanji 重訂南漢誌. By Hong Kyŏng-mo 洪敬謨. Manuscript. N.d.

Dabanruo boluomiduo jing 大般若波羅蜜多經. Woodblock. Fuzhou: Kaiyuan si, printed from blocks carved in 1115 and repaired between 1341 and 1368.

Dafoding shoulengyan jing shujie mengchao 大佛頂首楞嚴經疏解蒙鈔. Annot. Qian Qianyi 錢謙益. Manuscript. Handwritten by Qian in the 17th cent.

Daihannya haramitta-kyō 大般若波羅蜜多経. Woodblock. Kasuga-ban. Nara, early 13th cent.

Daihannya haramitta-kyō 大般若波羅蜜多経. Woodblock. N.p., 1384.

Dai Nihon dōchū kōtei saikenki 大日本道中工程細見記. By Torikai Dōsai 鳥飼洞齋. Woodblock. Osaka: Kichimonjiya Ichibee; Edo: Kichimonjiya Jirobee, 1770.

Dai Nihon saiken dōchū zukan 大日本細見道中図鑑. By Tomonari Shōkyoku 友鳴松旭. Ed. Fujitani Tōyūshi 富士谷東遊子. Woodblock. Tōto [Tokyo]: Izumiya Ichibee, 1876.

"Damo mian bi tu bing zan" 達磨面壁圖並贊. By Fengdian 風顛. Rubbing of indeterminate date.

"Dayan ta Foke ji timing" 大雁塔佛刻及題名 (east lintel). Rubbing of indeterminate date, of engravings dating between 618 and 1580. (Bingham 5R-A1)

"Dayan ta Foke ji timing" 大雁塔佛刻及題名 (south lintel). Rubbing of indeterminate date, of inscriptions dating between 618 and 1634. (Bingham 5R-A3)

Donglai Lü taishi wenji 東萊呂太史文集. By Lü Zuqian 呂祖謙. Ed. Lü Qiaonian 呂喬年. Woodblock. N.p., 1204.

Ehon Tsurezuregusa 絵本徒然草. By Kenkō 兼好. Ill. Nishikawa Sukenobu 西川祐信. Woodblock. Kyoto: Kikuya Kihei, 1740.

Eiga monogatari 栄華物語. Movable type. N.p., 1624–43.

Ekiro no suzu 駅路乃鈴. Woodblock. [Kyoto]: Izumoji Izuminojō, 1709.

Fang shi mopu 方氏墨譜. Comp. Fang Yulu 方于魯. Woodblock. N.p.: Fang shi Meiyin tang, 1589.

Fūryū Shidōken den 風流志道軒伝. By Hiraga Gennai 平賀源内. Woodblock. Edo, 1763.

Futari minashigo 二人ミナシゴ. By Tengai 天外. Frontispiece by Kajita Hanko 梶田半古. Tokyo: Kinkōdō, 1903.

Geishi 鯨志. By Yamase Haruyasa 山瀬春政. Woodblock. Kyoto: Kōbunkan, 1760.

Genji kokagami 源氏小鏡. By Fujiwara Nagachika 藤原長親. Woodblock. Edo, n.d.

Genji monogatari 源氏物語. By Murasaki Shikibu 紫式部. Ed. Yamamoto Shunshō 山本春正. Woodblock. N.p., 1654.

Gezhi huibian 格致彙編 1, no. 10 (Nov. 1876).

Gui fan 閨範. By Lü Kun 呂坤. Ill. Huang Yingchun 黃應淳. Woodblock. N.p.: Boru zhai, 1590–1620.

Gu shi Yihai lou cang yinkuan niu tuoben 顧氏藝海樓藏印款紐拓本. Comp. Gu Yuan 顧沅. 19th-cent. rubbings and imprints of seals dating to the Ming and Qing dynasties.

Haedong kayo 海東歌謠. Ed. Kim Su-jang 金壽長. Manuscript. N.d.

"Haha" 母. By Akutagawa Ryūnosuke 芥川竜之介. Manuscript. 1921.

Hamyŏng 含英 [*Kyubang midam* 閨房美談]. Manuscript. N.d.

Hanjungnok 恨中錄. By Hyegyŏnggung Hong Ssi 惠慶宮洪氏. Manuscript. N.d.

Honglou meng tuyong 紅樓夢圖詠. Ill. Gai Qi 改琦. Woodblock. N.p.: Huaipu jushi, 1879.

Huaihai ji 淮海集. By Qin Guan 秦觀. Woodblock. Ming printing from blocks originally carved in Gaoyou, by Gaoyou junxue, in 1173.

Hwanghwa chip 皇華集. Woodblock. N.p., n.d.

Hwasŏng sŏngyok ŭigwe 華城城役儀軌. Metal movable type with woodblock. N.p., 1800.

Hyakumantō darani. Metal plate or woodblock. N.p., 764–70.

Hyakunin isshu zōsan shō 百人一首像讚抄. By Nakanoin Michikatsu 中院通勝. Ill. Hishikawa Moronobu 菱河師宣. Woodblock. Edo: Urokogataya, 1683.

Inhang ilgi 仁港日記. Manuscript. Ca. 1888.

Iphak tosŏl 入學圖説. By Kwŏn Kŭn 權進. Woodblock. Yŏngch'ŏn, 1547.

Isanatori ekotoba 勇魚取絵詞. By Oyamada Tomokiyo 小山田与清. Woodblock. Edo, 1829.

Jianben fuyin Chunqiu Gongyang zhushu 監本附音春秋公羊註疏. Woodblock. Guozijian ed. N.p. Ming printing from Yuan blocks.

Jiezi yuan huazhuan sanji 芥子園畫傳三集. By Wang Shi 王著, Wang Gai 王槩, Wang Nie 王臬. Woodblock. Reengraving of original ed. [Nanjing]: Jiezi yuan shengguan, 1796–1820.

Jujō Genji 十帖源氏. By Nonoguchi Ryūho 野々口立圃. Woodblock. N.d.

Kaitai shinsho 解體新書. By Johann Adam Kulmus. Trans. Sugita Genpaku 杉田玄白. Woodblock. Tōbu [Edo]: Subaraya Ichibee, 1774.

Kanje sijip 簡齋詩集. By Chen Yuyi 陳與義. Woodblock. N.p., 1544.

Kita Ezo zusetsu 北蝦夷図説. By Mamiya Rinzō 間宮林蔵 and Hata Sadayasu 秦貞廉. Ill. Hashimoto Gyokuransai [Sadahide] 橋本玉蘭齋 [貞秀] and Shigeta Tansai 重探齋. Edo: Harimaya Katsugorō, 1855.

Kōkei saikyūhō 廣恵濟急方. By Taki Motonori 多紀元徳. Ed. Taki Motoyasu 多紀元簡. Woodblock. [Edo]: Suharaya Kasuke et al., 1790.

Konjiki yasha 金色夜叉. By Ozaki Kōyō 尾崎紅葉. Frontispiece by Takeuchi Keishū 武内桂舟. Tokyo: Shun'yōdō, 1898.

Korō monogatari 古老物語. By Torii Kiyostune 鳥居清経. Ill. Torii Kiyotsune. Woodblock. [Edo: Urokogataya, n.d.]

Koshoku zuki 耕織図. By Lou Shou 樓璹. Ill. Lou Shou. N.p.: Sokendo, 1676.

Kūmo kyech'ŏp 金吾禊帖. Manuscript. 1745–1805.

Kurofune raikō Uraga okatame no zu 黒船来航浦賀固メ之図. Manuscript. Ca. 1853.

Kyō warabe 京童. By Nakagawa Kiun 中川喜雲. Woodblock. Kyoto: Tamamori Rokubei, 1658.

Lienü zhuan 列女傳. By Liu Xiang 劉向. Ed. Wang Daokun 汪道昆. Ill. attr. Qiu Ying 仇英. Woodblock. N.p.: Zhibuzu zhai, 1779.

Li Zhuowu xiansheng piping Xixiang ji 李卓吾先生批評西廂記. By Wang Shifu 王實甫. Ed. Li Zhi 李贄. Woodblock. N.p.: Liu Yingxi, after 1573.

Meriken shinshi 米利軒新誌. By Tsurumine Shigenobu 鶴峰戊申. Ill. Gyokuransai Sadahide 玉蘭斎貞秀. Woodblock. N.p.: Kasugaru, 1855.

Myōhōrengekyō 妙法蓮華経. Manuscript. N.d.

Myōjō shō 明星抄. By Yosano Akiko 与謝野晶子. Ill. Hirafuku Hyakusui 平福百穂. Printed by Nishimura Kumakichi 西村熊吉. Woodblock. Tokyo: Kanao Bun'endō, 1918.

Nagasaki saiken no zu 長崎細見の図. Woodblock. Nagasaki: Bunkindō, 1851.

Nansō Satomi hakkenden 南総里見八犬伝. By Kyokutei Bakin 曲亭馬琴. Ill. Yanagawa Shigenobu 柳川重信. Woodblock. Osaka: Kawachiya Shigeru Hyōe; Edo: Yōrokuya Heibee, 1823.

Nanzenbushū bankoku shōka no zu 南瞻部洲万国掌菓之図. By Hōtan 鳳潭. Woodblock. Keichō [Kyoto]: Bundaiken Uje, 1710.

Narita meisho zue 成田名所図会. By Nakaji Sadatoshi 中路定得 and Nakaji Sadanori 中路定堤. Ill. Hasegawa Settei 長谷川雪堤. Woodblock. [Narita]: Shinshō shōja, 1858.

"Nei Gong li" 内公鬲. Ca. 19th-cent. rubbing of bronze dating to 1027–256 BC.

Nihon kaisan chōrikuzu zu 日本海山潮陸図. By Ishikawa Ryūsen 石川流宣. Woodblock. Edo: Sagamiya Tahee, 1694.

Nihon meisho no e 日本名所の絵. By Keisai Shōshin [Kitao Masayoshi] 蕙齋紹真 [北尾政美]. Woodblock. N.p., 1803.

Nise Murasaki inaka Genji 偽紫田舎源氏. By Ryūtei Tanehiko 柳亭種彦. Ill. Utagawa Kunisada 歌川国貞 and Utagawa Toyokuni 歌川豊国. Woodblock. Tōto [Edo]: Tsuruya Kiemon, 1829–42.

Oracle bone fragment. Shang dynasty.

Oranda shinyaku chikyū zenzu 喎蘭新譯全図. By Hashimoto Sōkichi 橋本宗吉. Woodblock with hand-coloring. Keishi [Kyoto]: Ogawa Tazaemon et al., 1796.

Peiwen zhai Gengzhi tu 佩文齋耕織圖. By Lou Shou 樓璹, Qing Shengzu 清聖祖, Qing Shizong 清世宗. Ill. Jiao Bingzhen 焦秉貞. Tokyo: Tōyōdo, 1892.

Qinding gujin tushu jicheng 欽定古今圖書集成. Comp. Chen Menglei 陳夢雷 and Jiang Tingxi 蔣廷錫. Bronze movable type and woodblock. Beijing: Wuying dian, 1726.

[*Qisheng yanhai tu* 七省沿海圖]. Manuscript. After 1787.

Rangaku kaitei 蘭学階梯. By Ōtsuki Gentaku 大槻弦沢. Woodblock. Osaka: Gungyokudō, 1788.

Rikka hiden shō 立花秘伝抄. Woodblock with hand-coloring. Kyoto, 1688.

Samgang haengsilto 三綱行實圖. Comp. Kye Sun 偰循. Woodblock. P'yŏngyang, 1726.

Sekaizu narabini Nihonzu byōbu 世界図並日本図屏風. Screen. 1640.

Senken nagaya 千軒長屋. By Shimamura Hōgetsu 島村抱月. Frontispiece by Kaburaki Kiyokata 鏑木清方. Tokyo: Josandō, 1908.

Shenyin jiangu lu 審音鑑古錄. Woodblock. N.p.: printed before 1834, from blocks of uncertain date.

Shizhu zhai shuhua pu 十竹齋書畫譜. Ed. Hu Zhengyan 胡正言. Woodblock. N.p.: Haiyang Hu shi, 17th cent.

Shūi Miyako meisho zue 拾遺都名所図絵. By Akizato Ritō 秋里籬島. Ill. Takehara Shunchōsai 竹原春朝齋. Woodblock. [Kyoto]: Yoshinoya Tamehachi, 1787.

Sibo kongsin hoemaengmun 十五功臣會盟文. Metal and wooden movable type. N.p., early 17th cent.

Sōkka yōrae haengjŏk song 釋迦如來行跡頌. Attr. Wuxue 無學. Woodblock. N.p., 15th cent.

Suizoku shashin 水族写真. Comp. and ill. Okugura Tatsuyuki 奥倉辰行. Color woodblock. Tōto [Edo]: Suiseidō, 1855.

Suruga no kuni Fujisan ezu 駿河国富士山絵図. Woodblock. N.p., 18th cent.

Su Wenzhong gong wenji 蘇文忠公文集. By Su Shi 蘇軾. Woodblock. Meishan, 1126–1279.

Taebanya paramilta kyŏng 大般若波羅蜜多經. Woodblock. Hapch'ŏn, printing of indeterminate date from blocks engraved in 1238.

Taedong yŏjido 大東輿地圖. By Kim Chŏng-ho 金正浩. Woodblock with added color. N.p.: [Kim], 1861.

Taehak yŏnŭi 大學衍義 and *Chinsōsan toksōgi ulchipsang taehak yŏnŭi* 真西山讀書乙集上大學衍義. By Zhen Dexiu 真德秀. Movable type. N.p., 17th cent.

Taiheiki 太平記. Wooden movable type. N.p.: Shunshi kaiban, 1610.

Teikan zusetsu 帝鑑図説. By Zhang Juzheng 張居正 and Lü Diaoyang 呂調陽. Woodblock. [Kyoto]: Yao Sukezaemon, 1650.

Tōkaidō-chū hizakurige 東海道中膝栗毛. By Jippensha Ikku 十返舎一九. Ill. Jippensha et al. Woodblock. N.p., 1865?

Tōkaidō gojūsantsugi michi annai 東海道五十三驛道案内. By Akatsuki Kanenari 暁鐘成. Woodblock. Osaka: Shioya Kihei, 1844.

Tōkaidō gyōretsu sugoroku 東海道行列双六. Ill. Gountei Sadahide 五雲亭貞秀. Engr. Tanaka Tetsuya 田中鉄弥 and Tanaka Ushinosuke 田中牛之助. Woodblock. Edo: Itoya Shōbee, 1860.

Tōkaidō narabini Saigoku dōchū emaki 東海道並西国道中絵巻. Manuscript. 1700.

Tōkaidō narabini Saigoku dōchū ezu 東海道並西国道中絵図. By Komaki Minō 古牧美農. Manuscript. 1687.

Tōto meisho zue 東都名所図絵. By Saitō Chōshū 齋藤長秋. Ill. Hasegawa Settan 長谷川雪旦. Woodblock. Tokyo: Subaraya Ihachi, 1834–36.

Unha kyŏnmunnok 雲下見聞錄. By Kim Kyu-rak 金奎洛. Manuscript. Ca. 1871.

Wubei zhi 武備志. By Mao Yuanyi 茅元儀. Woodblock. N.p., 1621.

Wudai shi quewen 五代史闕文. By Wang Yucheng 王禹偁. Manuscript. Hand-copied by Peng Yuanrui 彭元瑞 in 1787.

Xianfo qizong 仙佛奇蹤. By Hong Yingming 洪應明. Woodblock. N.p., Ming dynasty.

Xinke liandui bian meng tuxiang Qibao gushi daquan 新刻聯對便蒙圖像七寶故事大全. By Wu Daoming 吳道明. N.p., Huang Cibai, Jiyi tang, 1604.

Xinqin quanxiang dazi tongsu yanyi Sanguo zhizhuan 新鋟全像大字通俗演義三國志傳. By Luo Guanzhong 羅貫中. Woodblock. Jianyang: Qiaoshan tang, 1573–1644.

"Xiping shijing canshi" 熹平石經殘石. Ca. 19th-cent. rubbing of inscription dating to AD 175.

Xiqing shihua 西清詩話. Attr. Cai Tao 蔡絛. Manuscript. Hand-copied between 1368 and 1644.

Xixiang ji 西廂記. By Wang Shifu 王實甫. Ill. attr. Qiu Ying 仇英. Callig. attr. Wen Zhengming 文徵明. Manuscript. N.d.

Yaqu cangshu 雅趣藏書. By Qian Shu 錢書. Woodblock. N.p.: Chongwen tang, preface dated 1703.

"Yarong jun hufu" 壓戎郡虎符. Ca. 19th-cent. rubbing of bronze tally dating to AD 9–25.

Yi fu ji 易附記. By Weng Fanggang 翁方綱. Manuscript. Ca. 1800.

Yi Hyŏn-gyŏng chŏn 이현경전. Manuscript. 1912.

Yŭhai 玉海. Comp. Wang Yinglin 王應麟. Woodblock. N.p.: Qingyuan lu ruxue, 1340.

Yuming xinci sizhong 玉茗新詞四種. By Tang Xianzu 湯顯祖. Ed. Zang Maoxun 臧懋循. Woodblock. N.p.: Diaochong guan, 1618.

Zatsudan amayo no shichigura 雑談雨夜質庫. By Tamenaga Shunsui 為永春水. Ill. Utagawa Kunisato 歌川國郷 and Utagawa Kunihisa 歌川國久. Woodblock. Edo: Wakasa Yoichi, 1856–61.

"Zhang Tianshi xiang bing zan" 張天師像并贊. Rubbing of indeterminate date, of stone relief dating to 756–63.

Zhongyi shuihu zhuan 忠義水滸傳. By Shi Nai'an 施耐庵. Annot. Li Zhi 李贄. Woodblock. N.p.: Jiezi yuan, 1600–27.

SOURCES CITED

1. BEFORE THE BLOCK-PRINTED BOOK

Keightley, 3, 18–23, 46, 136, 140; Li, 3–6, 53–60; Xiao, 2–3, 42–47—Fang 1998, 21; Gan, "Yin zheng fushuo," 2a/b; Huang 1994, 4; Tsien 1962, 54–57—Carter, 19; Shaanxi bowuguan et al., 26; Tsien 1962, 74–78, 86–87—Chibbett, 29, 32; Kornicki, 116; Nakane, 9–10; Sansom 1958, 86–91.

2. WOODBLOCK IMPRINTS

Shi, 117; Tsien 1985, 197; Wei 1988, 71–76—Bokelai Jiazhou daxue Dongya tushuguan, no. 606; Fang 1969, 30.7; *Seikadō bunko Sō-Gen-ban zuroku* 2:64–65; Shi, 119–20; Tsien 1985, 201; Wei 1988, 47–49; Wei and Wang, 120—Chibbett, 41, 59–60, 94–96; Gardner, 157–59; Kornicki, 118–19; Ōya, 85; Sansom 1958, 135—Bokelai Jiazhou daxue Dongya tushuguan, no. 35; Nagasawa, 259, 263; *Seikadō bunko Sō-Gen-ban zuroku* 2:143; Tsien 1985, 177, 215–16; Wang 1998, 8.96; Wei 1988, 43–45, 94–97, 145—Fang 1969, 28.26; Sohn 1971, 32–33; Tsien 1985, 322–25; Twitchett and Tietze, 111–12; Zhang 1989, 766—Feng, 34, 67; Shih, 38–40; Tsien 1985, 253; Zhang 1989, 547; Zheng 1957, 7; Zhou, 103, 106.

3. VARIATIONS IN PRINT

Fang 1969, 5.4, 6.1; Lee et al. 1996, 536–39; Sohn 1971, 34–35, 39–40, 43; Su 2:1598–1600—Chibbett, 70–72, 76; Fang 1969, 19.29; Kawase 1:351, 1:542–43, 2:5; Kornicki, 126, 130–31, 134; Satow, 2:3:66; Sohn 1959, 101; Tsien 1985, 221, 326–27, 330—Kawase 2:13; Kornicki, 134–35; Matsumura 1:308; Nakata, 106—Chibbett, 118–19; Kanada, 12–13; Kornicki, 58; Yamashita, 13—Chibbett, 35–36; Feng, 86–89; Tschichold, 14; Zhang 1989, 568–69—Chibbett, 75–76; Irie, 26; Johnson, 248–50, 256–59; Ogino, 1–2.

4. PRINTING FOR A POPULAR AUDIENCE

Bokelai Jiazhou daxue Dongya tushuguan, no. 422; Chia, 44, 142–43, 185–88, 289; Zhang 1989, 59, 377— Lü; Chia, 207; Tsien 1985, 261, 263; Zheng 1974, 585–86; Zheng 1985, 193—Kato, 185–88, 233–34; Kornicki, 239–42; Leutner, 125n46; Sakanishi, 185–86; Sansom 1963, 32–34, 187, 200—Forrer, 33, 71; Chibbett, 79, 231, 303; Keene, 428–34; Kornicki, 170, 340, 343; Leutner, 8—Kornicki, 165–66; Merritt and Yamada, 4–5, 13, 201–2; *Nihon shuppan bunkashiten '96 Kyōto zuroku*, 66–67, 130.

5. TRANSMISSION OF TEXTS

Bokelai Jiazhou daxue Dongya tushuguan, nos. 516, 733; Goodrich, 17n3, 42–43, 47–49, 61, 100–103, 104n7, 147, 186—Fang 1969, 22.29; Haboush 1992, 31; Haboush 1996, 4–5, 31–35—Bokelai Jiazhou daxue Dongya tushuguan, nos. 12, 16, 20; Fang 1969, no. 19.15; Fang 1944, 857; Shen, 407—Bokelai Jiazhou daxue Dongya tushuguan, nos. 130, 750; Fang 1969, 30.6; Tuotuo et al., 231.13727; Zhang 2002, "Qianyan," 10–14—Bokelai Jiazhou daxue Dongya tushuguan, nos. 447, 598; Tsien 1985, 220–21.

6. THE THREE TEACHINGS

Ban, 36.1957; Bokelai Jiazhou daxue Dongya tushuguan, no. 408; Fang 1976a, 1:210; Fang 1976c, 1:1007; Ji 2:1264, 1854; Murray 2005, 427; Wu 1590–1620, 1b; Zhou, 227—Kalton, 107–9; Osgood, 247–48; Kim 1871, 36a, 37b—Bokenkamp, 143; Ji, 3:3002—Muroga and Unno, 51, 62, 69; Miyake, 171–74—Mowry and Berliner, 309; Murray 1994, 137; Wu 1950, 452.

7. COURT, TOWN, AND COUNTRY

Morris, 161; Murase, 4–6; Sakanishi, 179; Sansom 1958, 178, 194—Fang 1969, 19.9, 19.41; Clark and Clark, 35–36, 149–50; Portal, 124–26—Akizato, [1b–2a]; Béranger, 100–101; Chibbett, 127–28; Kawata, 48–49; Levy and Sneider, 13, 141–42; Munemasa, 78–79; Matsudaira 1834–36, [1]—Asahiyama, 2b–3a; Hawley, 21, 208, 217, 229, 265; Kaempfer, 77–78; Kalland and Moeran, 68–71, 152; Kumano Taijiura hogeishi hensan iinkai, 290—Hummel, 274–77; Kuhn, 336–39; Laufer, 98–101; Lou 1676, [1a/b]; Lou 1913–17, 8.12a–13b; Monnet, 12–14, 19–20.

8. THE PURSUIT OF PLEASURE

Chance, 68–69; Chibbett, 90, 130; Matsudaira 1988, 176–78; Yoshida, 3, 9, 12—Bokelai Jiazhou daxue Dongya tushuguan, no. 778; Chia, 241–42; He, 11, 69–70; Zang, 4a; Chao, 1–2, 6–8, 18–21; Togari, *passim*; Wang 1930, 114, 130–31—Blacker, 593–94; Formanek, 167–68; Hall, 363, 365–66, 371–72; Traganou, 12–14, 22; Vaporis, 25–26—Fang 1969, 37.6, 40.9; Kim 2003, 250–60; Lee 2003a, 168–70; Lee 2003b, 119; Lee 2003c, 220; Sang, 1.1a–2a, 14a—"Dayan ta Foke ji timing" (north, south, east, west lintels); Wang 2003, 3.53–54, 3.80; Zhang 1922, 1b–2a; Zhao, 7.14a.

9. FOREIGN EXCHANGE

Bowers, ix, 11–16, 29–31, 70–71, 92–95; Boxer, 47–49; Jansen, 92; Ogawa, 55, 59; Rudolph, 107; Sansom 1963, 35–45, 116; Sugimoto and Swain, 322–23—Béranger, 103; Bowers, 103, 120–21, 124–25; Brown, 289; Howard, 39, 51–52, 67; Mamiya, 55ff., 64ff.; Ōtani, 106–11; Ohnuki-Tierney, 90–96; Stephan, 36–39—Fang 1969, 19.39; Haboush 1996, 25; Henderson, 378–82; Kim 1997, 65; Lee et al. 1993, 106; Needham and Wang, 215–18, 220; Ji, 3:2398–99; Unesco World Heritage Committee, 61–63—Bennett, 4, 17, 25, 29, 51–52; Chang, 10–12; Dagenais, Preface; Spence, 141, 147, 152–54; Wang 2000, 121–22.

10. MAPPING LAND AND SEA

Bokelai Jiazhou daxue Dongya tushuguan, no. 206; Fang 1976b, 636–37; Huang 1976, 204–8; So, 19—Clark and Clark, 49–53; Ledyard, 301–2, 324–29, 337—Miyazaki, 344–46; Yamashita, 9, 13, 49, 107—Muroga, 161, 164–65; Unno, 410; Yee, 177, 186.

BIBLIOGRAPHY

Akizato Ritō. 1787. "Jijo." In *Shui Miyako meisho zue*, by Akizato. [Kyoto]: Yoshinoya Tamehachi.

Asahiyama Kanjō. 1760. "Jo *Geishi*." In *Geishi*, by Yamase Haruyasa. Kyoto: Kōbunkan.

Ban Gu. 1963. *Han shu*. Beijing: Zhonghua shuju.

Bennett, Adrian Arthur. 1967. *John Fryer: The Introduction of Western Science and Technology into Nineteenth-Century China*. Harvard East Asian Monographs, no. 24. Cambridge: East Asian Research Center, Harvard University, Harvard University Press.

Béranger, Veronique. 2002. "Les recueils illustrés de lieux célèbres (*meisho zue*), objets de collection: Leur réception dans les milieux de la Société des études japonaises à travers l'exemple de la collection d'Auguste Lesouëf (1829–1906)." *Ebisu* 29:81–113.

Blacker, Carmen. 1984. "The Religious Traveller in the Edo Period." *Modern Asian Studies* 18:593–608.

Bokelai Jiazhou daxue Dongya tushuguan, ed. 2005. *Bokelai Jiazhou daxue Dongya tushuguan Zhongwen guji shanben shuzhi*. Shanghai: Shanghai guji chubanshe.

Bokenkamp, Stephen. 1986. "Taoist Literature, Part I: Through the T'ang Dynasty." In *The Indiana Companion to Traditonal Chinese Literature*, ed. William H. Nienhauser et al., 138–52. Bloomington: Indiana University Press.

Bowers, John Z. 1970. *Western Medical Pioneers in Feudal Japan*. Baltimore: Johns Hopkins Press.

Boxer, C. R. 1950. *Jan Compagnie in Japan, 1600–1850*. 2nd rev. ed. The Hague: Martinus Nijhoff.

Brown, Yu-Ying. 1990. "Byways in Japanese Illustration." In *Japanese Studies*, ed. Brown, 277–96. British Library Occasional Papers 11. London: The British Library.

Carter, Thomas Francis. 1955. *The Invention of Printing in China and Its Spread Westward*. Rev. by L. Carrington Goodrich. 2nd ed. New York: The Ronald Press.

Chance, Linda H. 1997. *Formless in Form: Kenkō, Tsurezuregusa, and the Rhetoric of Japanese Fragmentary Prose*. Stanford: Stanford University Press.

Chang Hao. 2004. "Chinese Terms for Chemical Elements: Characters Combining Radical and Phonetic Elements." *Chemistry International* 26, no. 1 (Jan.–Feb.): 10–13.

Chao Guanzhi. 1936. *Mojing. Congshu jicheng* ed. Shanghai: Shanghai yinshuguan.

Chia, Lucille. 2002. *Printing for Profit: The Commercial Publishers of Jianyang, Fujian (11th–17th Centuries)*. Cambridge: Harvard University, Asia Center for Harvard-Yenching Institute.

Chibbett, David. 1977. *The History of Japanese Printing and Book Illustration*. Tokyo: Kodansha International Ltd.

Clark, Allen D., and Donald N. Clark. 1969. *Seoul, Past and Present: A Guide to Yi T'aejo's Capital*. Seoul: Hollym Corporation, Royal Asiatic Society, Korea Branch.

Dagenais, Ferdinand. 2004. Preface to *John Fryer's Berkeley Years: Documents Illustrating His Life and Tenure as First Agassiz Professor of Oriental Languages and Literature, 1986–1914*, ed. Dagenais. Typescript.

"Dayan ta Foke ji timing." Rubbings of indeterminate date, from inscriptions dating 618–1634. Bingham 5R–A1, 5R–A2, 5R–A3, 5R–A4, East Asian Library, University of California, Berkeley.

Fang, Chaoying. 1944. "Wêng Fang-kang." In *Eminent Chinese of the Ch'ing Period (1644–1912)*, ed. Arthur W. Hummel, 2:856–58. Washington, D.C.: Government Printing Office.

———. 1969. *The Asami Library*. Berkeley and Los Angeles: University of California Press.

———. 1976a. "Cheng Kuei-fei." In *Dictionary of Ming Biography*, ed. L. Carrington Goodrich and Fang, 1:208–11. New York and London: Columbia University Press.

———. 1976b. "Hu Tsung-hsien." In *Dictionary of Ming Biography*, ed. L. Carrington Goodrich and Fang, 1:631–38. New York and London: Columbia University Press.

———. 1976c. "Lü K'un." In *Dictionary of Ming Biography*, ed. L. Carrington Goodrich and Fang, 1:1006–10. New York and London: Columbia University Press.

Fang Zonggui. 1998. *Zhongguo yinzhang shi*. Taibei: Shuxiang chubanshe.

Feng Pengsheng. 1999. *Zhongguo muban shuiyin gaishuo*. Beijing: Beijing daxue chubanshe.

Formanek, Susanne. 1998. "Pilgrimage in the Edo Period: Forerunner of Modern Domestic Tourism? The Example of the Pilgrimage to Mount Tateyama." In *The Culture of Japan as Seen through Its Leisure*, ed. Sepp Linhart and Sabine Frühstück, 165–93. Albany: State University of New York Press.

Forrer, Matthi. 1985. *Eirakuya Tōshirō, Publisher at Nagoya: A Contribution to the History of Publishing in 19th Century Japan*. Japonica Neerlandica, vol. 1. Amsterdam: J. C. Gieben.

Gan Yang. 1596. *Jigu yinpu*. N.p.

Gardner, K. B. 1990. "Centres of Printing in Mediaeval Japan: Late Heian to Early Edo Period." In *Japanese Studies*, ed. Yu-Ying Brown, 157–69. British Library Occasional Papers 11. London: The British Library.

Goodrich, Luther Carrington. 1935. *The Literary Inquisition of Ch'ien-lung*. American Council of Learned Societies Studies in Chinese and Related Civilizations, no. 1. Baltimore: Waverly Press, Inc.

Haboush, JaHyun Kim. 1992. "The Texts of the *Memoirs of Lady Hyegyŏng*: The Problem of Authenticity." *Gest Library Journal* 5:29–48.

Haboush, JaHyun Kim, trans. and annot. 1996. *The Memoirs of Lady Hyegyŏng: The Autobiographical Writings of a Crown Princess of Eighteenth-Century Korea*. Berkeley: University of California Press.

Hall, Robert B. 1937. "Tokaido: Road and Region." *Geographical Review* 27:353–77.

Hawley, Frank. 1959. *Whales and Whaling in Japan*. Miscellanea Japonica II. Kyoto.

He, Yuming. 2003. "Productive Space: Performance Texts in the Late Ming." Ph.D. diss., University of California, Berkeley.

Henderson, Gregory. 1957. "Chŏng Ta-san: A Study in Korea's Intellectual History." *Journal of Asian Studies* 16:377–86.

Howard, B. Douglas. 1893. *Life with Trans-Siberian Savages*. London: Longmans, Green, and Co.

Huang Dun. 1994. *Zhongguo gudai yinlun shi*. Shanghai: Shanghai shuhua chubanshe.

Huang, Stanley Y. C. 1976. "Cheng Juo-tseng." In *Dictionary of Ming Biography*, ed. L. Carrington Goodrich and Chaoying Fang, 1:204–8. New York and London: Columbia University Press.

Hummel, Arthur. 1929. "Accessions to the Division of Chinese Literature." *Annual Report of the Librarian of Congress for the Fiscal Year 1927–28*, 274–77. Washington, D.C.: Government Printing Office.

Irie Haruyuki. 1957. *Yosano Akiko shoshi*. Osaka: Sogensha.

Jansen, Marius. 2000. *The Making of Modern Japan*. Cambridge: Belknap Press of Harvard University Press.

Ji Yun, ed. 1933. *Siku quanshu zongmu tiyao*. Shanghai: Shangwu yinshuguan.

Johnson, Scott. 1990. "*Shasei ryokō* and the 'Sketch Tour' Books of the Early 20th Century." In *Japanese Studies*, ed. Yu-Ying Brown, 248–60. British Library Occasional Papers 11. London: The British Library.

Kaempfer, Englebert. 1999. *Kaempfer's Japan: Tokugawa Culture Observed*. Ed., trans., and annot. Beatrice M. Bodart-Bailey. Honolulu: University of Hawai'i Press.

Kalland, Arne, and Brian Moeran. 1992. *Japanese Whaling: End of an Era?* Scandinavian Institute of Asian Studies Monograph Series, no. 11. Richmond, Surrey: Curzon Press.

Kalton, Michael C. 1985. "The Writings of Kwŏn Kŭn: The Context and Shape of Early Yi Dynasty Neo-Confucianism." In *The Rise of Neo-Confucianism in Korea*, ed. Wm. Theodore de Bary and JaHyun Kim Harboush, 89–123. New York: Columbia University Press.

Kanada, Margaret Miller. 1989. *Color Woodblock Printmaking: The Traditional Method of Ukiyo-e*. Tokyo: Shufunotomo Co.

Kato Shuichi. 1997. *A History of Japanese Literature, from the Man'yōshū to Modern Times*. Trans. and ed. Don Sanderson. New abr. ed. Richmond, Surrey: Japan Library.

Kawase Kazuma. 1967. *Kokatsujiban no kenkyū*. Tokyo: Nihon koshosekisho kyokai.

Kawata Hisashi, ed. 1990. *Edo meisho zue o yomu*. Tokyo: Tōkyōdō shuppan.

Keene, Donald. 1976. *World within Walls: Japanese Literature of the Pre-modern Era, 1600–1867*. New York: Grove Press.

Keightley, David N. 1978. *Sources of Shang History: The Oracle-Bone Inscriptions of Bronze Age China*. Berkeley: University of California Press.

Kim Hŏnggyu. 2003. "Chosŏn Poetry in Chinese." In *A History of Korean Literature*, ed. Peter H. Lee, 250–60. Cambridge: Cambridge University Press.

Kim Kwang-on. 1997. "Instruments of the Hwasong Wall Construction Process." In *Hwasŏng sŏngyok ŭigwe sŏp'yŏng mŏumjip*, ed. Lee Jong-Hak, 65–69. Suwŏn: Saye Yŏnguso.

Kim Kyu-rak. Ca. 1871. *Unha kyŏnmunnok*. Manuscript. Asami 15.14, East Asian Library, University of California, Berkeley.

Kornicki, Peter. 2001. *The Book in Japan: A Cultural History from the Beginnings to the Nineteenth Century*. Honolulu: University of Hawai'i Press.

Kuhn, Dieter. 1976. "Die Darstellungen des Keng-chih-t'u und ihre Wiedergabe in populär-enzyklopädischen Werken der Ming-Zeit." *Zeitschrift der Deutschen Morgenländischen Gesellschaft* 126:336–67.

Kumano Taijiura hogeishi hensan iinkai, ed. 1969. *Kumano Taijiura hogeishi*. Tokyo: Heibonsha.

Laufer, Berthold. 1912. "The Discovery of a Lost Book." *T'oung Pao* ser. 2, 13:96–106.

Ledyard, Gari. 1987. "Cartography in Korea." In *Cartography in the Traditional East and Southeast Asian Countries*, vol. 2, book 2 of *The History of Cartography*, ed. J. B. Harley and David Woodward, 235–345. Chicago: University of Chicago Press.

Lee, Peter H. 2003a. "Early Chosŏn *sijo*." In *A History of Korean Literature*, ed. Lee, 168–88. Cambridge: Cambridge University Press.

———. 2003b. "Koryŏ Writings in Chinese." In *A History of Korean Literature*, ed. Lee, 118–47. Cambridge: Cambridge University Press.

———. 2003c. "Late Chosŏn *sijo*." In *A History of Korean Literature*, ed. Lee, 201–27. Cambridge: Cambridge University Press.

Lee, Peter H., et al., eds. 1993. *Sourcebook of Korean Civilization*, vol. 1, *From Early Times to the Sixteenth Century*. New York: Columbia University Press.

———. 1996. *Sourcebook of Korean Civilization*, vol. 2, *From the Seventeenth Century to the Modern Period*. New York: Columbia University Press.

Leutner, Robert W. 1985. *Shikitei Sanba and the Comic Tradition in Edo Fiction*. Harvard-Yenching Institute Monograph Series 25. Cambridge, Mass., and London: Council on East Asian Studies, Harvard University, and the Harvard-Yenching Institute.

Levy, Dana, and Lea Sneider. 1983. *Kanban: Shop Signs of Japan*. New York: Weatherhill.

Li Xueqin. 2000. *Jiagu bainian hua cangsang*. Shanghai: Shanghai keji jiaoyu chubanshe.

Lou Shou. 1676. *Koshoku zuki*. N.p.: Sokendo.

Lou Yao. 1913–17. "Ba Yangzhou bofu gengzhi tu." In *Gongkui tiba*, by Lou. *Shiyuan congshu* ed.

Lü Xianfu. 1787. "Fanli." In *Chanzhen yishi*, by Fang Ruhao. N.p.

Mamiya Rinzō. 1981. *Tōdatsu kikō*. Higashimurayama: Kyōikusha.

Matsudaira Sadatsune. 1834–36. Foreword to *Tōto meisho zue*, by Saitō Chōshū. Tokyo: Subaraya Ihachi.

Matsudaira Susumu. 1988. *Moronobu Sukenobu ehon shoshi*. Musashimurayama-shi: Seishōdō shoten.

Matsumura Hiroji, ed. 1969–82. *Eiga monogatari zenchūshaku*. Tokyo: Kadokawa shoten.

Merritt, Helen, and Nanako Yamada. 2000. *Woodblock Kuchi-e Prints: Reflections of Meiji Culture*. Honolulu: University of Hawai'i Press.

Miyake, Toshiyuki. 1987. "Sutra Mounds." In *Art of the Lotus Sutra: Japanese Masterpieces*, ed. Bunsaku Kurata and Yoshirō Tamura, and trans. Edna B. Crawford, 171–74. Tokyo: Kōsei Publishing Co.

Miyazaki Fumiko. 2005. "Female Pilgrims and Mt. Fuji: Changing Perspectives on the Exclusion of Women." *Monumenta Nipponica* 60:339–91.

Monnet, Nathalie. 2003. *Le Gengzhitu, le livre du riz et de la soie; poèmes de l'empereur Kangxi, peintures sur soie de Jiao Bingzhen*. Paris: JC Lattès.

Mowry, Robert, and Nancy Berliner. 1994. "Guanyin Sutra." In *Latter Days of the Law: Images of Chinese Buddhism, 850–1850*, ed. Marsha Weidner, 309–11. Lawrence: Spencer Museum of Art, University of Kansas; Honolulu: University of Hawai'i Press.

Munemasa Isō, ed. *Kyō no meisho zue o yomu*. Tokyo: Tōkyōdō shuppan, 1998.

Murase, Miyeko. 1983. *Iconography of the Tale of Genji: Genji monogatari ekotoba*. New York and Tokyo: Weatherhill.

Muroga Nobuo. 1973. "The Development of Cartography in Japan." In *Old Maps in Japan*, ed. Nanba Matsutarō, Muroga, and Unno Kazutaka, and trans. Patricia Murray, 158–76. Osaka: Sogensha.

Muroga Nobuo and Unno Kazutaka. 1962. "The Buddhist World Map in Japan and Its Contact with European Maps." *Imago Mundi* 16:49–69.

Murray, Julia K. 1994. "The Evolution of Buddhist Narrative Illustration in China after 850." In *Latter Days of the Law: Images of Chinese Buddhism, 850–1850*, ed. Marsha Weidner, 125–49. Lawrence: Spencer Museum of Art, University of Kansas; Honolulu: University of Hawai'i Press.

———. 2005. "Didactic Illustrations in Printed Books." In *Printing and Book Culture in Late Imperial China*, ed. Cynthia J. Brokaw and Kai-wing Chow, 417–50. Berkeley: University of California Press.

Nagasawa Kikuya. 1934. "Genkanbon kokukō meihyo shokō." *Shoshigaku* 2:257–68.

Nakane Masaru, ed. 1987. *Hyakumantō darani no kenkyū*. Osaka: Hyakumantō darani no kenkyū kankō iinkai.

Nakata, Yujiro. 1973. *The Art of Japanese Calligraphy*. Trans. Alan Woodhull and Armins Nikovskis. New York and Tokyo: Weatherhill/Heibonsha.

Nanba Matsutarō. 1973. "The Pleasures of Collecting Old Maps." In *Old Maps in Japan*, ed. Nanba, Muroga Nobuo, and Unno Kazutaka, and trans. Patricia Murray, 146–57. Osaka: Sogensha.

Needham, Joseph, and Wang Ling. 1965. *Physics and Physical Technology: Mechanical Engineering*, vol. 4, pt. 2 of *Science and Civilisation in China*, ed. Needham. Cambridge: Cambridge University Press.

Nihon shuppan bunkashiten '96 Kyōto zuroku. 1996. Tokyo: Nihon shoseki shuppan kyōkai.

Ogawa Teizō. 1968. *Kaitai shinsho; Rangaku o okoshita hitobito*. Tokyo: Chūō kōronsha.

Ogino Yasushige. 1992. *Yosano Akiko Myōjō shō no kenkyū*. Tokyo: Ōfūsha.

Ohnuki-Tierney, Emiko. 1974. *The Ainu of the Northwest Coast of Southern Sakhalin*. New York: Holt, Rinehart and Winston, Inc.

Osgood, Cornelius. 1951. *The Koreans and Their Culture*. New York: The Ronald Press Company.

Ōtani Tsunehiko, ed. 1982. *Mamiya Rinzō no saihakken*. Tsuchiura-shi: Tsukuba Shorin.

Ōya Tokujō. 1923. *Nara kangyō shi*. Kyoto: Naigai shuppan.

Portal, Jane. 2000. *Korea: Art and Archaeology*. New York: Thames and Hudson.

Rudolph, Richard C. 1966. "Illustrated Botanical Works in China and Japan." In *Bibliography and Natural History: Essays Presented at a Conference Convened in June 1964*, ed. Thomas R. Buckman, 103–20. University of Kansas Publications, Library Series 27. Lawrence: University of Kansas Libraries.

Sakanishi, Shio. 1941. "Notes on Japanese Accessions." In *Annual Report of the Librarian of Congress for the Fiscal Year Ended June 30, 1940*, 174–88. Washington, D.C.: Government Printing Office.

Sang Shichang. 1821. *Huiwen leiju*. N.p.: Linyu tang.

Sansom, George. 1958. *A History of Japan to 1334*. Stanford: Stanford University Press.

———. 1963. *A History of Japan, 1615–1867*. Stanford: Stanford University Press.

Satow, Ernest Mason. 2001. "On the Early History of Printing in Japan." In *Collected Works of Ernest Mason Satow*, pt. 2, vol. 3. London: Ganesha Publishing.

Seikadō bunko Sō-Gen-ban zuroku. 1992. Tokyo: Seikadō bunko, Kyūko shoin.

Shaanxi bowuguan et al., eds. 1983. *Xi'an Beilin shufa yishu*. [Xi'an]: Shaanxi renmin meishu chubanshe.

Shen Jin. 2002. *Weng Fanggang nianpu*. Zhongguo wenzhe zhuankan 24. Taibei: Zhongyang yanjiuyuan, Zhongguo wenzhe yanjiusuo.

Shi Tingyong. 1987. *Zhongguo guji banben gaiyao*. Ed. Zhang Xiumin. Tianjin: Tianjin guji chubanshe.

Shih, Hsio-yen. 1958. "On Ming Dynasty Book Illustration." M.A. thesis, University of Chicago.

So, Kwan-wai. 1975. *Japanese Piracy in Ming China during the 16th Century*. N.p.: Michigan State University Press.

Sohn, Pow-key. 1959. "Early Korean Printing." *Journal of the American Oriental Society* 79:96–103.

———. 1971. *Early Korean Typography*. Seoul: Korean Library Science Research Institute.

Spence, Jonathan D. 1969. *To Change China: Western Advisers in China, 1620–1960*. Boston: Little, Brown and Company.

Stephan, John J. 1971. *Sakhalin: A History*. Oxford: Clarendon Press.

Su Shi. 1999. "Shang Zhezong lun Gaoli ren shi mai shu." In *Songchao zhuchen zouyi*, ed. Zhao Ruyu, 2:1598–1600. Shanghai: Shanghai guji chubanshe.

Sugimoto, Masayoshi, and David L. Swain. 1978. *Science and Culture in Traditional Japan, AD 600–1854*. Cambridge: MIT Press.

Togari Soshinan. 1953. *Tōhoku Waboku zusetsu*. [Tokyo]: Bijutsu shuppansha.

Traganou, Jilly. 2004. *The Tōkaidō Road: Traveling and Representation in Edo and Meiji Japan*. New York and London: RoutledgeCurzon.

Tschichold, Jan. 1953. *Chinese Color-Prints from the Painting Manual of the Mustard Seed Garden*. New York: The Beechhurst Press.

Tsien, Tsuen-Hsuin. 1962. *Written on Bamboo and Silk: The Beginnings of Chinese Books and Inscriptions*. Chicago: University of Chicago Press.

———. 1985. *Paper and Printing*, vol. 5, pt. 1 of *Science and Civilisation in China*, ed. Joseph Needham. Cambridge: Cambridge University Press.

Tuotuo et al. 1977. *Song shi*. Beijing: Zhonghua shuju.

Twitchett, Denis, and Klaus-Peter Tietze. 1994. "The Liao." In *Alien Regimes and Border States, 907–1368*, ed. Herbert Franke and Twitchett, 43–153, vol. 6 of *The Cambridge History of China*, ed. Twitchett and John. K. Fairbank. New York: Cambridge University Press.

Unesco World Heritage Committee. "Advisory Body Evaluation." http://whc.unesco.org/archive/advisory_body_evaluation/817.pdf.

Unno, Kazutaka. 1987. "Traditional Japanese Cartography." In *Cartography in the Traditional East and Southeast Asian Countries*, vol. 2, book 2 of *The History of Cartography*, ed. J. B. Harley and David Woodward, 346–477. Chicago: University of Chicago Press.

Vaporis, Constantine N. 1997. "To Edo and Back: Alternate Attendance and Japanese Culture in the Early Modern Period." *Journal of Japanese Studies* 23:25–67.

Wang Chi-chen. 1930. "Notes on Chinese Ink." *Metropolitan Museum Studies* 3:114–33.

Wang Dingbao. 2003. *Tang Zhiyan jiaozhu*. Ed. Jiang Hanchun. Shanghai: Shanghai shehui kexue yuan chubanshe.

Wang Pu, ed. 1998. *Wudai huiyao*. Beijing: Zhonghua shuju chubanshe.

Wang Yangzong. 2000. *Fu Lanya yu jindai Zhongguo de kexue qimeng*. Beijing: Kexue chubanshe.

Wei Yinru. 1988. *Zhongguo guji yinshua shi*. Beijing: Yinshua gongye chubanshe.

Wei Yinru and Wang Jinyu. 1984. *Guji banben jianding congtan*. Beijing: Yinshua gongye chubanshe.

Wu, K. T. 1950. "Chinese Printing under Four Alien Dynasties." *Harvard Journal of Asiatic Studies* 13:447–523.

Wu Yunqing. 1590–1620. "Ke *Gui fan* yin." In *Gui fan*, by Lü Kun. N.p.: Boru zhai.

Xiao Ai. 1980. *Jiaguwen shihua*. Beijing: Wenwu chubanshe.

Yamashita Kazumasa. 1998. *Japanese Maps of the Edo Period, Chizu de yomu Edo jidai*. Trans. Charles De Wolf. Tokyo: Kashiwashobo.

Yee, Cordell D. K. 1987. "Traditional Chinese Cartography and the Myth of Westernization." In *Cartography in the Traditional East and Southeast Asian Countries*, vol. 2, book 2 of *The History of Cartography*, ed. J. B. Harley and David Woodward, 170–202. Chicago: University of Chicago Press.

Yoshida Kenkō. 1967. *Essays in Idleness: The Tsurezuregusa of Kenkō*. Trans. Donald Keene. New York and London: Columbia University Press.

Zang Maoxun. 1618. "Yuming tang chuanqi yin." In *Yuming xinci sizhong*, by Tang Xianzu, ed. Zang. N.p.: Diaochong guan.

Zhang Bowei, ed. 2002. *Xijian ben Songren shihua sizhong*. Nanjing: Jiangsu guji chubanshe.

Zhang Li. 1922. *You chengnan ji. Baoyan tang miji* ed.

Zhang Xiumin. 1989. *Zhongguo yinshua shi*. Shanghai: Renmin chubanshe.

Zhao Han. 1921. *Moji juan hua. Zhibuzu zhai cong shu* ed.

Zheng Zhenduo. 1957. *Jiezhong de shu ji*. Shanghai: Gudian wenxue chubanshe.

———. 1974. "Zhongguo banhua xuan xuyan." In *Zhongguo tushu shi ziliao ji*, ed. Liu Jiabi, 585–87. Hong Kong: Longmen shudian.

———. 1985. "Zhongyi shuihu zhuan chatu ba." In *Zheng Zhenduo meishu wenji*, ed. Zhang Qiang, 193–95. Beijing: Renmin meishu chubanshe.

Zhou Xinhui. *Zhongguo gudai banke banhua shi lunji*. Beijing: Xueyuan chubanshe, 1998.

AUTHOR'S ACKNOWLEDGMENTS

This book is wholly dependent on the contributions of others—the printers and copyists, book collectors, librarians, and friends responsible for producing the books now in the East Asian Library's rare book rooms, for preserving them, and for bringing them to Berkeley. More directly, the author is indebted to Jean Han, Jaeyong Chang, and Yuki Ishimatsu, of the East Asian Library, for their help in selecting the images that appear in these pages; to Jae Chang and Jianye He, of the Library, for reading the manuscript in draft; to Bruce Williams, Tomoko Kobayashi, and Evelyn Kuo, of the Library, for favors of all kinds; to Peter Zhou, Director of the Library, for his enthusiastic support of the project; to Diana Chen, of SF Digital Studio, Inc., for her eye, expertise, and generosity; and to Malcolm Margolin and the staff at Heyday, for their patience in guiding the book from incipit to print.

ABOUT THE C. V. STARR EAST ASIAN LIBRARY

Formally established in 1947, the East Asian Library of the University of California, Berkeley, offers one of the most comprehensive collections of Chinese, Japanese, and Korean materials in the United States. The Library is central to research and teaching in the field of East Asian studies on campus and is highly respected internationally. Its comprehensive collections document the history, culture, and social and economic development of China, Japan, and Korea from ancient to contemporary times. Some of its individual collections are unparalleled outside of East Asia. Its rare holdings include early imprints, manuscripts, rubbings, and maps; its digital collections include electronic books, online journals, and full-text databases. Renamed in 2007, the C. V. Starr East Asian Library serves faculty and students of the university, residents of the state of California, and scholars from around the world.

ABOUT THE AUTHOR

Deborah Rudolph is senior editor at the East Asian Library. She holds a Ph.D. in classical Chinese from the University of California, Berkeley, and a Master's in library science from UCLA. Both her father and her husband's father collected early Japanese and Chinese imprints.

ABOUT THE PHOTOGRAPHER

Diana Chen contributed both her photography and design skills to *Impressions of the East*. An alumna of the University of California, Berkeley, Diana is founder of SF Digital Studio, Inc., in San Francisco, a state-of-the-art digital photography studio specializing in commercial and archival imagery.